Wandering into Grace

Wandering into Grace
A Journey of Discovery and Hope

978-1-5018-9626-2
978-1-5018-9627-9 eBook

Laurie Haller

Wandering into Grace

A Journey of Discovery and Hope

Abingdon Press / Nashville

Wandering into Grace

Copyright © 2020 Abingdon Press

All rights reserved.

Library of Congress Control Number: 2019955031

978-1-5018-9626-2

Scripture quotations unless noted otherwise are taken from the Common English Bible, copyright 2011. Used by permission. All rights reserved.

Scripture quotations noted (NRSV) are from New Revised Standard Version Bible, copyright © 1989 National Council of the Churches of Christ in the United States of America. Used by permission. All rights reserved worldwide. http://nrsvbibles.org/

Scripture quotations marked MSG are taken from *THE MESSAGE*, copyright © 1993, 1994, 1995, 1996, 2000, 2001, 2002 by Eugene H. Peterson. Used by permission of NavPress. All rights reserved. Represented by Tyndale House Publishers, Inc.

Scripture quotations marked (NIV) are taken from the Holy Bible, New International Version®, NIV®. Copyright © 1973, 1978, 1984, 2011 by Biblica, Inc.™ Used by permission of Zondervan. All rights reserved worldwide. www.zondervan.com The "NIV" and "New International Version" are trademarks registered in the United States Patent and Trademark Office by Biblica, Inc.™

20 21 22 23 24 25 26 27 28 29 — 10 9 8 7 6 5 4 3 2 1

MANUFACTURED IN THE UNITED STATES OF AMERICA

Contents

Introduction

"Wandering" is not a waste of time. Wandering is essential to the understanding of our faith. Was it not Moses, leading his people in the wilderness, who proclaimed, "A wandering Aramean was my ancestor" (Deuteronomy 26:5 NRSV)? This declaration, even self-realization, became a defining credo of the Hebrews, who wandered for forty years in the desert before crossing over the Jordan River. Abraham was a wanderer. Jacob was a wanderer. I know that I am also a wanderer. However, I have never felt that I've wandered aimlessly. Rather, I've always had the conviction that I am wandering ever deeper into God's grace.

I suspect that I began wandering into grace before I was even born, for I was always surrounded by love. Jesus called me as a child because of the example of my mother and father and the influence of the Mennonite church in which I grew up. I was undergirded from my earliest years by the prayers of my parents, grandmothers, and church members who nurtured my faith. From loving Sunday school, to reading books from the church library, to seeing God's handiwork by wandering the woods and fields around my home, to taking lessons on the church organ, to attending Bible studies with my grandmother, to giving the sermon on Youth Sunday, my church nurtured me in grace and instilled a quest for God that has never left me. And Jesus? He kept calling me.

Jesus kept calling me even though women were not permitted to be ordained in the Mennonite Church USA when I was growing up. Jesus kept calling me, even though no one ever encouraged me to consider pastoral ministry. After all, what would be the point? Jesus kept calling me, even though I never even met a clergy-woman until I was in graduate school. Still, Jesus kept calling me to wander into grace, for it is God who formed my inward parts and knit me together in my mother's womb.

It has only been within the past several years that I have found the word that fits who I am spiritually. I used to call myself a pilgrim, who is on a continuous journey into the heart of God and is led by the spirit toward holy destinations. But now I realize that I am really a *peregrina*.

Peregrinatio is a Latin word that comes from Roman law and refers to living, sojourning, or wandering outside of one's homeland with no specific destination. In Celtic Christianity, some *peregrini* were exiled to other countries because they broke laws, but other *peregrini* voluntarily chose to spend their lives in foreign lands, away from family and friends. Some of these so-called "white martyrs" were seeking personal fulfillment, but others engaged in missionary endeavors. Saint Columba, who left his home in Ireland out of a self-imposed penance, founded a monastic community on the holy island of Iona and converted most of Scotland and England to Christianity.

Jesus has called me to be a *peregrina*, to move outside my people, the Mennonites, to the once-foreign land of The United Methodist Church, and then to the episcopacy. And because of John Wesley, I now realize that the whole world is my parish, and all people are my people! As an itinerant preacher, my life has no destination other than to wander into grace, model the suffering love of Jesus, seek justice and reconciliation, offer hope to The United Methodist Church, and work to bring in God's reign on this earth.

In July 2018, I began a two-month renewal leave from my ministry as the episcopal leader of the Iowa Annual Conference of The United Methodist Church. I had been elected and consecrated as a bishop in August 2016 and hit the ground running on September 1. It didn't take long to realize that I would never last in this position unless I was proactive in caring for myself. United Methodist bishops are mandated to take leave time every four years in order to rest and renew body, mind, and spirit. I could not do this ministry without such a time of renewal.

Spending my first week at Conception Abbey, a Benedictine Abbey in Missouri, I yearned to read, write, reflect, and worship. I brought with me *A Guide to Retreat for All God's Shepherds*, by Bishop Rueben Job, a book that I used for my two previous leaves in 2001 and 2011. Interestingly, Bishop Job served as the episcopal leader of Iowa, where I now serve, from 1984 to 1992. Job's book has been invaluable in identifying my own spiritual emptiness and leading me toward a healthier way of living and being in ministry.

I came to Conception Abbey in order to "come apart," to leave my home and regular setting to be able to see God more clearly and be more attentive to God's still, small voice. Job quotes Evelyn Underhill about listening to the One "who has nothing to learn from you but everything to tell you."[1]

I wrote in my journal,

> I am here to worship and sing with the monks and hear the voice of God. I will listen and be attentive to what God has for me. When I come away, I realize how empty I am. There is nothing to mask the silence, the despair, the loneliness. Yet, I can hear you very clearly, God, and I know that you are near. I know that you love me. I know that I am enveloped in your

grace. I need to rediscover the power of your witness. I am totally dependent upon you.

I need to remember that when all I hear is silence, God is still there. I think about what lies ahead for the future of our church, and all I hear is silence. Still, I wonder. What will become of us? What will become of my friends if our church splits? I have so many friends on both sides of the divide. Will I lose them? What do I need to give up? What do I have to place in your hands, God? I worry about the witness we will make to the world if we can't find a way to live together and honor and even celebrate our differences.

Is dividing the church worth being right? I continue to knock, seek, pray, wonder, love, serve, and honor the differences. I relinquish all to you, God. I surrender all.

The rhythms of Conception Abbey nurtured my spirit. I decided to forego Vigils at 6 a.m. because of my need for sleep. I did, however, attend Lauds at 7:15 a.m., Eucharist at 11:45 a.m., Daytime prayer at 1 p.m., Vespers at 5:15 p.m., and Compline at 7:15 p.m. I was disappointed not to be able to receive the sacrament at Conception Abbey because I am not Catholic. Unfortunately, however, life soon intervened, and I became preoccupied by other matters.

On the second full day, as I was running through the Missouri prairie, I wandered into trouble instead. Deciding to run on a trail with heavy grass, I soon tripped over a hidden root and fell on my left wrist. I came apart literally. I sensed immediately that the injury was serious, so I turned around and ran back to the retreat center.

Just as Jesus went into the desert at the beginning of his

ministry and was ministered to by angels, so a staff member at Conception Abbey graciously came to my aid when I could not help myself. This angel drove me to the nearest hospital a half hour away, where an X-ray revealed a fractured wrist. I left with pain meds, a splint for my hand and wrist, and instructions to see an orthopedist as soon as I arrived back home.

I spent the rest of the week in silence with the monks, foregoing the pain meds so that I would be fully alert to the promptings of the Spirit. As Kathleen Norris writes in *Dakota: A Spiritual Geography*,

> Silence is the best response to mystery. "There is no way of telling people," Merton reminds us, "that they are all walking around shining like the sun." New Yorkers are told a great many things by strangers on the street, holy fools and mad alike. But the monk's madness is one that shows in the quiet life itself, with its absurd repetition of prayer and liturgy. It is the "madness of great love," in the words of one monk, that "sees God in all things," which nevertheless may be safely and quietly carried out of the monastery, into the world, and back again. As Basil Cardinal Hume, a Benedictine, has remarked, the monk is safe in the marketplace because he is at home in the desert.[2]

I was devastated to think that my best-laid plans for renewal may have already been thwarted since I was planning to leave for a trek in Nepal a week later. However, I came to believe that through this injury, God was slowing me down from the frenetic pace of a bishop as well as teaching me humility and grace in preparation for all the learning that was to come. Participating with the monks in the daily cycle of prayer helped to anchor me spiritually during this first week of decompression from years of intense ministry with few extensive breaks.

From the beginning of my renewal leave, I had to learn how to empty myself, let go of all expectations, and live in a continual sense of gratitude. I came to realize that other people will enrich my life if I surrender and allow them to become angels of grace for me. In the same way, as a leader who is also a Christ follower and *peregrina*, I am walking with and for others on the journey.

Our *peregrina/peregrino* God continues to call each one of the faithful to wander our world for such a time as this, as witnesses to God's redemptive grace, agents of hope, and bearers of the light of Christ. This Holy Wanderer tenderly invites us to come home to the heart of God by living in unity and freely offering shalom to our beautiful, frightening, and glorious world.

Wandering into Grace shares my story of discovery and hope on the high Himalayan trails of Nepal in the summer of 2018. If you're searching for me now, you'll probably find this *peregrina* wandering the roads and prairies of Iowa and the world, going wherever the Spirit leads and sharing the grace of Jesus Christ.

The God who has searched me and known me, the Holy One who knows when I sit down and when I rise up, the Creator who has fearfully and wonderfully made each one of you, the original *Peregrina/Peregrino* who continues to search our path and has led each one of us to this place—it is this God who continues to wander our world: calling, forming, shaping, weeping, listening, serving, suffering, and offering grace through you and through me. May we continue to wander with this God of grace.

Chapter
1

Waiting has always been one of the most challenging spiritual disciplines for me. . . . When I have been forced to wait, I have often considered it to be wasting time rather than "waiting for the Lord." Whenever I have been tempted to give up or give in to despair, I have remembered the words of the prophet Isaiah.

Chapter 1
Reflect, Adjust, Do

I have always been up for a challenge. Maybe that's why our first grandson used to call me Crazy Grandma! Having been a pastor for thirty-eight years, I have encountered almost everything in my ministry. I have been pushed and pulled in different directions. I have been challenged to the max in dealing with difficult situations that stretch my faith and cause me to doubt. I have been chastised, rebuked, and vilified for a variety of reasons. And I have been forgiven and deeply loved more than I will ever deserve.

Because ministry is such an intense calling, I have pursued an "alternate" life ever since I started pastoring my first church on January 1, 1982. I made a commitment to care for my mind, body, and spirit so that I would not burn out. Oddly, as I have grown older and my ministry settings have become more demanding, I have chosen to pursue physical and mental challenges that stretch my endurance, challenge my abilities, and confirm my craziness. No matter where I find myself, however, I discover that I am wandering into grace.

I was sitting in a hotel room in Nepalgunj, a large town in central Nepal, on a warm July day, waiting with my daughter Talitha and pondering to myself, "Why am I doing this, anyway?" A year before, I had talked with her about pursuing an adventure together, knowing that I had set apart some renewal leave time in the summer of 2018. We were both in good shape and were compatible travelers. We had two and a half weeks and said, "Let's go on a trek in Nepal!" Trekking in Nepal seemed like a great option because we both loved to hike, travel, and experience different parts of our beautiful world.

How strange was it that I broke my wrist less than a week before departing to Nepal? What was God telling me? Perhaps this: "You are a wounded healer, Laurie. And risk is part of your life. On this leave, you will carry both your pain and your decision not to be afraid."

I wondered why I was doing this, anyway, especially with my broken wrist. There were so many things that could go wrong. The risks caused anxiety, but I needed to push myself mentally and physically, just as I have been continually challenged in my role as a bishop in The United Methodist Church. I have been constantly learning about myself and my limits, about when to stretch and speak out, and when to hold back. Even when others have taken offense or criticized, I have remained committed to showing grace, yet I have needed to be true to myself as well. My flaws have kept me humble and centered in Christ. The broken wrist also reminded me of the help that I had received and continued to need from others. My time of solitude at Conception Abbey was deep and rich. No one knew who I was. But I knew. I am a *peregrina* and a pilgrim and am open to continual transformation.

Arriving in Kathmandu from the United States, the sights, sounds, and sensations of the capital city of Nepal immediately put me on overload: narrow streets, most unpaved, and people everywhere walking, riding bikes or motorbikes, and driving wherever they wanted. It was pure chaos! Kathmandu is one of the fastest-growing and most polluted cities in Asia. The pollution was visible, hanging in the air like a dark mist. The Bagmati River ran through the city like a streaming sewer, and the majority of Kathmandu residents wore face masks, for good reason. Pollution resulted from ongoing infrastructure projects, emissions from industries, and a lack of green space where all of the dust could land and be absorbed. Garbage was everywhere, and the current infrastructure simply could not keep pace with the influx of residents.

Talitha and I were more than ready to head off into the mountains. We had worked for months with a tour operator to do the fourteen-day Lower Dolpo Trek in the isolated western part of Nepal. However, after flying from Kathmandu to Nepalgunj and overnighting, we discovered that our flight into Juphal had been canceled because of high winds and rain. In fact, a plane had crashed at Juphal the week before in bad weather, but our tour operator in Kathmandu somehow neglected to inform us of the situation. After waiting four hours in this one-room airport packed with other travelers, we went back to the hotel for another night.

Waiting has always been one of the most challenging spiritual disciplines for me. I have not been very patient and have seemed to fly through life in a hurry. When I have been forced to wait, I have often considered it to be wasting time rather than "waiting for the Lord." Whenever I have been tempted to give up or give in to despair, I have remembered the words of the prophet Isaiah.

Why do you say, O Jacob,
and speak, O Israel,
"My way is hidden from the LORD,
and my right is disregarded by my God"?
Have you not known? Have you not heard?
The LORD is the everlasting God,
the Creator of the ends of the earth.
He does not faint or grow weary;
his understanding is unsearchable.

He gives power to the faint,
  and strengthens the powerless.
Even youths will faint and be weary,
  and the young will fall exhausted;
but those who wait for the LORD shall renew their strength,
  they shall mount up with wings like eagles,
they shall run and not be weary,
  they shall walk and not faint.

(Isaiah 40:27-31 NRSV)

Little did I know that more than once in the next two weeks, I would "wait for the Lord" to renew my strength as I grew weary and sore from walking.

In the midst of this time of confinement to the hotel, I read and reflected upon other times when I had no choice other than to wait for the Lord. In the summer of 2011, I was beginning my last year as a district superintendent in the West Michigan Conference of The United Methodist Church. I was very aware of the impending transition as I took a three-month renewal leave. Early in the leave, I traveled to Ghost Ranch in New Mexico for a weeklong spiritual growth experience called "High Desert Spiritual Quest." Since being outside in nature is essential to my well-being, I was attracted by the mission statement of Ghost Ranch: "The Ranch is committed to spiritual development, peace and justice, honoring the environment, and exploring family through the celebration of art, culture and nature."[3]

The Ranch is a 21,000-acre retreat and education center of the Presbyterian Church in north central New Mexico. Ghost Ranch was also the home and studio of Georgia O'Keeffe, one of the first female painters to be recognized around the world. I distinctly remember my prayers during that week: "God, I don't know what's next for me after my last year as a district superintendent. My heart, mind, and spirit are open to your leading. All I want is to be your servant. What do you want me to do next with my life?"

Eight people from around the country were part of this group. My intention was to center myself in Christ. Through taking solitary hikes in the desert, participating in group exercises in trust-building, walking the Labyrinth, and studying scripture, my new friends helped me reframe the question. It was no longer, "God, what do you want me to do after my time as a superintendent is finished?" Rather, the question became, "God, wherever you call me next, who do you want me to be?"

I took off my shoes at Ghost Ranch and stood on holy ground, convinced that most important for my future was not what I was going to do but who I was going to be. However, that realization didn't guarantee smooth sailing, as I waited to see what God had in store for me next. I knew that as part of the appointive cabinet of the West Michigan Conference, the bishop was the one who would appoint me. I could only offer these words, "Here I am, Lord."

The following eight months of waiting were the greatest test of faith, hope, and love that I have ever experienced. My husband, Gary, would likely be staying at the church that we had served together for thirteen years and that he had continued to lead for the six years I was a superintendent. Unfortunately, there were not many options for me unless we decided to live apart, serving churches in different communities. My hope was that I could be appointed to a church where I could make use of the experience and gifts I had for ministry.

I distinctly remember when the cabinet first began discerning a new appointment for me in January 2012. I was excused as the cabinet began their conversation. My appointment was not finalized for several months, but what I remember the most was a serendipitous email that a friend sent to me on the first day my appointment was discussed.

He was recommending Richard Rohr's 2011 book, *Falling Upward: A Spirituality for the Two Halves of Life*. Rohr, a Franciscan priest, relies on the work of Carl Jung, who described the spiritual life in two stages. In the first stage, we humans seek to establish ourselves by discerning our life's work, creating an identity, surrounding ourselves with family and friends, and becoming successful.

In the second half of life, we come to the realization that there is more to life than recognition and financial security. There is also a deep yearning for meaning, spiritual connection, and wholeness. But that transition usually entails some sort of falling. The time will come in all of our lives when there is a crisis. It could be health issues, problems with children, the end of a relationship, loss of a job, or addiction. The reality of human life is that we don't always get what we deserve. Rather than "falling from grace," however, Rohr sees this stage as an opportunity to "fall upward," to begin to live with humility and thankfulness and let go of everything that prevents fullness of life.[4]

I was reminded of the words of Paul Brunton (1898–1981), a British theosophist and spiritualist who traveled the world exploring spiritual traditions. One of his best-known quotations is, "Many who ask for Grace would be shocked to hear that the troubles which may have followed their request were actually the very form in which the higher power granted the Grace to them."[5]

Could it be that I was encountering a "falling upward" from a "first half of life" into a "second half of life"? During those months of waiting for a new appointment, I wrestled mightily with God and finally allowed myself to fall upward into grace and hope. The appointment I received in 2012 was to two small churches that had been struggling, one urban and the other suburban. I fell upward into a beautiful and amazing year of ministry that was one of the most gratifying and hope-filled experiences I've ever had as a pastor.

Sitting in our hotel room when not pacing the hallways, I reflected on my own helplessness. I marveled at how odd it was that I broke my wrist a week before departing for Nepal. My wrist still bothered me, even though I was wearing a splint twenty-four hours a day. I also experienced limitations. I could barely write because I was left-handed, I couldn't put my backpack in the overhead bin by myself, and I was developing trigger finger from the splint.

What was God telling me? Was it time to slow down? Was this another "falling upward" moment? Did I need to discover a different way of working and serving that would not destroy my body or spirit?

I was choosing to see my broken wrist as a constant reminder that I was a wounded healer and that my wounds kept me humble and centered. I would carry with me for most of this leave the consequences of my decision to take a risk by running on the prairie. At the same time, I celebrated that risk is a vital part of my life and that I carried with me both my pain and my decision not to be afraid.

My musings also led me to examine the nature of how I make decisions. Strategic decision-making has always been a key component of my ministry. My time has been carefully scheduled, and I continually have to make difficult choices. I could not do everything and was always asking, "What is most important for me to do in my ministry as an episcopal leader?" I have tried to keep a careful and prayerful balance between conference and general church responsibilities. Communicating regularly with the conference and connecting personally with clergy and laity have also been high priorities.

At the same time, I have not been the kind of person who plays it safe all the time. I have not been afraid to risk in my personal and professional life and have wanted to stretch my limits and go for it. I like to balance the difficult challenges I face as a bishop with equally difficult (or some would say crazy) athletic challenges, like marathons, triathlons, long-distance bike rides, and this trek. So why was I sitting in a hotel room with nothing to do except read, walk the hallways, and wait for the weather to break?

On the second afternoon in the hotel, Talitha and I decided to take matters into our own hands, knowing that, otherwise, we might be stuck for days. We did a "RAD" on the situation. RAD, which stands for Reflect, Adjust, and Do, is a technique we have used in the Iowa Annual Conference to assess both our decisions and actions as a conference. For several years, we have contracted with Spiritual Leadership, Inc., for coaching in order to create healthier ministry environments.

At the end of every meeting of our various teams, we have always RADed our experience. What worked and what didn't? What do we need to let go of, add, or change? As Talitha and I assessed our situation, we decided that if we could not fly into Juphal the next day, we would instead fly back to Kathmandu and find another trek. Staying any longer in Nepalgunj would likely prevent us from doing any significant hiking elsewhere in Nepal.

Arriving very early at the airport the next day, we met two women who were also traveling to Dolpo. They said that if the flight was canceled again, we could rent a car and drive all night and possibly get to Dolpo this way. However, we would end up having to walk three hours with all our stuff to get into town. I forced myself to step back and wonder, *How is God teaching me at this moment?* We Americans have little tolerance for things that do not go as planned. The women explained that the Nepalese sense of time is much different from the American sense of time. The Nepalese do not have much money, but everything is much cheaper, and there is more time for leisure, going out to tea, chatting, and so forth.

Finally, we reached a tipping point. One of our new Nepalese friends helped us book a flight back to Kathmandu because we still hadn't heard from our tour operator. Others decided to rent vans and drive to Juphal. Still others remained in Nepalgunj to wait out the weather. As we prepared to board the plane to Kathmandu, we were asked to accompany a young female Buddhist monk who was on the same flight, and we were glad to travel with her. Reflect, adjust, do. Wise words for our journey through life.

On the flight back to Kathmandu, I reflected on the obstacles we were already facing on our Nepal adventure. How were we going to navigate through our canceled Lower Dolpo Trek, find a new trek, and execute it within the amount of time we had left in Nepal? We were not battling giants. We were, however, battling circumstances. Clearly, some of the issues were beyond our control. Despite the waiting and language, culture, and water/food challenges, however, we focused on creative problem solving and adaptive leadership, which were within our control. The story of David and Goliath came to mind. Even people who are not familiar with the Christian faith have heard this story of how David, an underdog who was only a shepherd boy, found a way to defeat a giant.

The Philistine nation had been seeking to expand into Israel for three generations and was a constant threat to the Israelites. In 1 Samuel 17, the Philistines were assembling their troops against King Saul and the Israelite army on opposite sides of a valley. A nine-foot-tall giant named Goliath came out of the Philistine camp to challenge the Israelites. His armor alone weighed 125 pounds, and the iron head on his spear weighed 15 pounds.

For forty days the Philistines took their stand. Meanwhile, Jesse, David's father, sent him to the Israelite camp with food for his brothers. At the same time, Saul made known that he was going to reward whoever killed Goliath.

David asked questions like, "How can he get away with insulting the army of the living God?"

King Saul responded, "You can't do this. You're just a boy!"

"Look," David said, "I fight lions and bears as a shepherd. What's the difference?"

"Then, go," Saul said, "and may the Lord be with you."

I could just imagine David doing a RAD on Goliath. He reflected on the situation, adjusted his strategy, and then did what he needed to do. King Saul proceeded to put his own armor on David, but it just wasn't comfortable. "I can't walk in this because I've never tried it before!" David exclaimed. Whereupon David took five smooth stones from the streambed and put them in his shepherd's bag. After mutual trash talk, David took a stone, slung it, and penetrated Goliath's forehead. Goliath fell facedown on the ground, and David finished him off with the giant's own sword.

In 2013, Malcolm Gladwell was interviewed for *Forbes* about his new book, *David and Goliath: Underdogs, Misfits, and the Art of Battling Giants*. Offering new insights into the biblical story of David and Goliath, Gladwell said,

> I started with the original story of David and Goliath because I became convinced that our interpretation of it was wrong; that it was a mistake to think of David as an underdog. He was simply someone rather who is using an alternate strategy and relying on his speed and his audacity, as opposed to size and strength, and I don't know why we think that.

We automatically assume that the biggest and strongest person at any contest is always the favorite. David was smarter, quicker, had the advantage of surprise and had an alternate strategy. Why doesn't that make him the favorite? The challenge is that the people who might appear to be underdogs or to be burdened with disadvantages actually aren't.[6]

Gladwell emphasized two lessons that we can take away from the story of David and Goliath. First, we humans can learn more from difficult times than good times, that there is opportunity in every crisis. He asserted, "I want people to understand that an incredible amount of what is beautiful and important in the world arises out of obstacles and adversity; that's the well from which a lot of what is beautiful springs in our world."[7]

The other takeaway is counterintuitive to much of what we have usually been taught: "The second thing is that we learn more from compensating for our weaknesses than capitalizing on our strengths. It's your weaknesses that define who you are and how you learn, and force you to do creative things, than making sense and working your way around your weaknesses, that we succeed."[8]

Clearly, Talitha and I were not engaging giants. Rather, we were confronting challenging circumstances where it was necessary to take the time to Reflect, Adjust, and Do. Despite the frustrations, we focused on positive problem solving.

We made the right decision to return to Kathmandu. After consulting with our tour operator, we decided to attempt the Manaslu Trek with a porter and a guide, just the four of us. In our original trek, we would have had four porters, donkeys to carry our food and tents, and even a cook. The level of complexity was now increased. I also realized that I was not totally comfortable with Manaslu since the trails were officially closed because of the rainy season. In addition, because we lost two days waiting in the hotel, we would have to eliminate the two built-in altitude acclimation days if we were to finish in the allotted time. It was our only realistic option, however.

The stunning Manaslu Circuit treks around Mount Manaslu, which, at 26,781 feet above sea level, is the eighth-highest mountain in the world. The Manaslu Circuit is known as the ultimate off-the-beaten-path trek in Nepal and is truly a remote adventure. It is in a region that was closed to outsiders until the early 1990s, and, still today, tourism is restricted. In fact, we did not encounter a single other trekker during our twelve days in the wilderness. And we did not see a single car during those days either.

The Manaslu Trek became more popular when teahouses began to be built along the way in 2010. The trail features everything one would expect from a great trek in Nepal, including epic scenery, many suspension bridges, and the Larkya Pass. The Manaslu Circuit allows trekking from March to June, and September to November. Somehow, Talitha and I were granted an exception to trek in July, and after the first day, I knew exactly why the Manaslu Circuit was usually closed at this time. It rained all night every single day. Absolute downpours! This meant that the trails, which were unmarked (one reason to require a guide), were a perpetual quagmire of slippery rocks, mud, and fast-moving streams. I realized this was very dangerous. The high point of the Manaslu Circuit is crossing the Larkya Pass at 17,060 feet, which is the highest elevation I have ever experienced.

Little did I know that we would have to make use of creative thinking and continuous adaption every day of our trek. Just as David engaged Goliath with courage and innovation, so we would have to engage the Manaslu Circuit as well as our own capabilities in the rainy season and at high altitude.

I was wary about the trip but had to let go of my anxiety. I had one good arm, and the other had a splint that was, I hoped, preventing my wrist from moving so that it could heal. But I looked forward to the adventure. The one thing I was sure of is that we would need to continuously RAD (reflect, adjust, do) our decisions. If our all-day trip to the start of the trek was any indication, we were going to be in for a wild ride.

Talitha and I received a duffel bag from the tour operator in the afternoon, and we were instructed not to take any more than what fit in our day packs and the porter's duffel that he would carry for us. The rest we would store at the hotel to be retrieved at the end of the trek.

As a bishop in The United Methodist Church, I was accustomed to packing because I travel a lot. I have a variety of packing lists depending on whether I am traveling for business, for a race, to visit family, or heading out of the country. I am particularly careful when traveling abroad to check and double check what's in my suitcase or backpack because it's not easy in remote areas to find what I might have forgotten. I've discovered from experience that I must carefully choose what to take and what to leave behind.

In the hotel lobby, we met Rajiv, our guide; Bishal, our porter; and the driver of the jeep that would take us to the start of the Manaslu Circuit in north central Nepal. After several hours of slow driving out of the Kathmandu metro area, we stopped for a break. It was midmorning, and I noticed that Rajiv, Bishal, and the driver were eating a big lunch. Meanwhile, Talitha and I walked around a little bit and took pictures. Amazingly, no one told us that this would be the only time we would stop for food until we reached the village at the start of the trek, which would be nine hours later. I bought three bottles of water, one for me, one for Talitha, and one for Rajiv.

Talitha and I had no idea what was in store for us! We soon began our ascent into the hills on narrow, winding mountain roads filled with ruts, huge boulders, and mud, mud, and more mud. Oh, and there were no guardrails. But the scenery was absolutely gorgeous! Lots of rice paddies and cornfields, beautiful vistas, and an occasional small village.

After five hours, we encountered a dump truck that was stuck in the mud in the middle of the road. Fortunately, it only delayed us for a half hour. It was fun watching our driver navigate the roads with a master's eye. It was the first of many times that I marveled at the skill of those who drove and guided us.

Twenty minutes later, high in the foothills of the Himalayas, after continuously escaping being mired in mud, we were flagged down by a farmer who warned us that there had been a landslide the night before, and the only road was impassable a half mile ahead. We drove until we reached the landslide, where it became clear that we could go no farther. This was, indeed, the only road, so we could not simply turn around and find another way.

We had no choice but to get out and walk. We emptied all our stuff out of the jeep and took stock of the situation. We had very little water, but we did have snacks. We put on our backpacks and said goodbye to our driver, who turned around and headed back to Kathmandu. Mind you, we had just met Rajiv and Bishal that morning. We didn't know one another very well, and it was brutally hot.

I innocently asked Rajiv, "How far do we have to walk to get to our destination?"

"I don't know," he replied. Oh my. This was not reassuring.

"Do you have GPS or a map, or can you make a phone call? It will be really helpful if we know how to manage our energy for the walk."

"There is no GPS or cell service here, and I don't have a map. I think we probably have a few kilometers to walk."

Hmmm. Somehow a few kilometers turned into ten kilometers (about six miles), over two hours of walking in the hot sun with fully loaded backpacks and virtually no water. After just a half hour, I told Rajiv that Talitha and I would not be able to go significantly farther without water. He said, "I'll check at the next farmhouse." The farm families were most willing to give us water, but it was tap water, and if we drank tap water, my daughter and I would surely become sick. All I had was one partially filled water bottle. Rajiv asked at each farmhouse until, finally, a family had a bottle of water that we purchased.

There was little talk as we walked. We were all lost in our own thoughts and were trying to conserve energy and avoid sunstroke. We finally arrived at a town where our guide wanted us to stay overnight. It was not our destination, however, and Talitha firmly insisted that we wait for the bus that would take us to the official start of our trek.

In retrospect, I realized that the harshness of our introduction to wilderness trekking was good preparation for the endurance and flexibility that would be demanded of us in the days ahead. Already, our experiences over the last four days had been amazing, and we hadn't even started the trek yet.

RAD for the day: It took a lot of patience, fortitude, waiting, and grit to even get to the beginning of our trek. As it often turns out, the journey itself is the destination. Fortunately, everywhere we turned, we were met with grace. The violent rush of water from the Budhi Gandaki River right outside our room at the teahouse quickly lulled us to sleep.[9] The adventure beckoned!

Chapter
2

What we were actually doing in our Come to Jesus meeting was employing the Rule of Christ that is laid out in Matthew 18. It should come as no surprise that the early church needed to develop procedures to address conflict resolution. . . . Along with the necessity of interacting with people of different races, cultures, religions, languages, and countries comes the inevitable challenge of honoring, accepting, and even loving differences.

Chapter 2
The Come to Jesus Meeting

It seemed almost impossible, but through many dangers, toils, and snares, we made it to the start of the Manaslu Trek and were more than ready to go. Our teahouse was right along the Budhi Gandaki River. Much of our 150-mile trek was along the powerful Budhi Gandaki, which becomes a raging river during the monsoon season. Precipitation is highest during July, exactly when we were there.

The teahouse where we slept was within feet of the Budhi Gandaki. The bathroom was in a small enclosed area outside, and there were squat toilets rather than sit-down toilets. A squat toilet pretty much consists of a deep hole in the ground or, if it is located in a building, a ceramic hole in the floor. It took some getting used to, but we cheerfully adapted.

After a breakfast of porridge, we were more than ready to get going but also realized that the four of us were now pretty much on our own for the next twelve days. Yes, we had concerns about a lack of communication from the trekking agency in relation to weather conditions and repeated canceled flights to Juphal. And no one kept us updated or contacted us while we waited at the airport. We were forced to proactively seek out natives of Nepal, particularly a young man who helped us negotiate and then rebook our flights back to Kathmandu.

I am convinced that leaders of organizations should always take the initiative to make sure their clients are safe and cared for, but Talitha and I were ready to put this behind us. We were learning how to negotiate in Nepal and hoping that our tour operator's ill-fated words from a December 2017 email, which we did not have in front of us when we rebooked the tour, would not be true for us: "I do not recommend doing Manaslu in monsoon, definitely not a good choice!"

I was intrigued by the Manaslu Circuit because it is a relative newcomer to the Nepal trekking world. Only two thousand visitors a year trek the Manaslu Circuit, thirty times less than the popular Annapurna Circuit. The first days of the trek follow the Budhi Gandaki River and climb three vertical miles. Suspension bridges give us opportunity to cross the river, and glaciers are found in the gorges. The trek passes through occasional villages and fields of barley, corn, and rice. The path is shared by herders with donkeys, traveling the same ancient route by which yaks have hauled salt from Tibet for centuries.

In reading about the Manaslu Trek, three cautions are raised. The first is the danger of sharing narrow mountain trails with donkeys. Because there are very few roads and even fewer cars in the mountains of Nepal, donkeys are used to carry supplies in and out of small villages, and everyone shares the same trails. We encountered groups of up to thirty donkeys dozens of times during our trek, and there are several guidelines for staying safe. When you hear the bells of the donkeys either behind or in front of you, stop immediately because donkeys and their herders have the right of way. Also, be sure to stop on the inside of the trail where there might be some extra space. Trekkers standing on the outside of the trail have been known to be blown off the mountain to their deaths either because of wind or because they were knocked off by a donkey. As you might imagine, there are no guardrails.

A second danger is cold and wind. Trekking in the summer does not present the same danger of low temperatures and ice that fall, winter, and spring trekking do. However, suitable clothing and trekking poles are essential for all seasons, with the addition of crampons in the winter.

The third danger is altitude, specifically, climbing too high too quickly. The farther we move away from sea level into higher altitudes, the lower the air pressure is. Our bodies can react in several ways to higher elevation and the corresponding lower air pressure. Air at a lower pressure contains less oxygen for each breath we take. Our bodies try to adjust by making more red blood cells to carry the oxygen cells more efficiently. However, this process takes time, so if we ascend a mountain too quickly, we may become ill.

That's why some of our trekking days on the Manaslu Circuit were shorter than others. Trekkers need time to acclimate to the next level of altitude. There are also occasions when the itinerary had us climbing higher, then walking back down to a lower altitude for the night in order for our lungs to adjust. Needless to say, altitude sickness must be taken very seriously because it can come on quickly and can be very debilitating. In addition, trekkers are usually at a distance from immediate help, and they are in a harsh environment where optimal health is essential.

Some physiological effects of altitude may be experienced by all people regardless of their health or ability. We tend to breathe faster at higher altitudes because we are compensating for the lower air pressure. We urinate more, may have interrupted breathing while sleeping, and tend to be dehydrated, therefore the need to keep drinking.

Rajiv was quite strict with us on making sure that we were always drinking to prevent dehydration. He asked how we were feeling and also followed protocols on how to more efficiently ascend to the Larkya Pass and descend on the other side. The two effects of altitude I experienced as we approached the Larkya Pass were sleep interruption and increased difficulty catching my breath.

Of course, there is one more danger of the Manaslu Circuit that is never mentioned in the guidebooks because the circuit is officially closed during the summer. Once we arrived at our official starting point, the first two days of the trek were very difficult because of the monsoon season. We had no choice but to go slow. Several times, the steep trail crossed creeks filled with mud and slippery rocks, and one time, Rajiv even insisted on carrying me across on his back. I wish had a picture of that adventure!

Another time, I slipped on a wet rock and scraped my elbow—a minor injury, to be sure, but an indication of the danger involved. Rajiv was especially mindful that my left hand was compromised because of my broken wrist, and I had to be careful about not putting my full weight on my left trekking pole, which was essential for balance.

After stopping for a soup lunch at a little village, it rained a bit, but we did not have to break out our rain pants and jackets. Eventually, we reached a "road" along the river, which was anything but level and smooth. It was a beautiful day, with no falls or incidents. But it was also very hard work and not for the out of shape or faint of heart. It was a nice surprise to end up on a little sandy beach along the river as we approached the village where we would spend the night.

The incredible beauty all around us was tempered by the necessity of always looking down. I had to concentrate completely on not falling because every surface was wet, slippery, and muddy. Talitha and I remarked that if the entire trek was going to be like this, it was going to be one miserable experience. I fell into my sleeping bag and was out like a light.

My mantra for the second day was *Focus*. It took an immense amount of concentration to avoid falling down, with millions of stones just waiting to trip us up. Navigating stones with many steps and engaging in continual uphill and downhill climbing, with lots of slick surfaces, demanded all of our strength and energy. Monsoon season trekking is inherently difficult, dangerous, and very messy, and as I got into the rhythm of trekking in the mud, I had to keep reminding myself to take the time to look around and enjoy the beautiful scenery.

Because it was the rainy season, most of the teahouses were closed, and there was limited eating. Today, an elderly woman was ready to make us lunch in a small village, but she was clearly not physically capable of cooking. So Rajiv and Bishal prepared our meal in her kitchen. They were both great cooks!

Our first crisis came immediately after lunch. I called it our "Come to Jesus" meeting, during which Talitha and I butted heads with our guide. A Come to Jesus moment or meeting may refer to a time when a person experiences a religious conversion or revelation and dedicates his or her life to Christ. However, the term has also taken on a more secular meaning. A Come to Jesus meeting or moment could refer to the time when a person realizes the need to make a life-altering decision. Or it could refer to a group meeting where difficult and transformative decisions must be made.

Before resuming our trek for the afternoon, Rajiv approached Talitha and me and expressed his apprehension about us being able to complete the entire trek in the time allotted. He was very complimentary about Talitha's abilities but was also concerned about my ability to make it through a thirteen-hour day later on in the trek when we crossed the Larkya Pass. He wondered if I was physically able to keep on because I had already slipped on a rock today and skinned an elbow.

I was incredulous! It is true that because we missed two days of hiking while waiting to do the Lower Dolpo Trek, we would have to combine two days of hiking into one thirteen-hour day. We would also need to eliminate a rest day meant to acclimate to the high altitude. Rajiv thought that it was unrealistic for me as an "older" person to accomplish this.

Talitha and I asked if there was another option other than simply turning around and backtracking, since the first day and a half had been utterly miserable. Neither Talitha nor I had it in us to redo the last two days. In addition, Talitha emphasized my ability to combine two days into one, saying that I was in far better physical condition than a typical woman my age. After all, a thirteen-hour day trekking was nothing compared to completing a thirteen-hour long-distance triathlon.

I asked Rajiv if the conditions of the trail would improve during the rest of the trip, and he said it would be just like the first two days all the way to the end. With the three of us at the table, we agreed to wait one more day to make a decision. However, Talitha and I had already decided that we would not turn around and redo the same hazardous trekking we had just accomplished.

Talitha and I were fully determined to complete the entire trek in twelve days rather than fourteen, including rest time to acclimate to the altitude. With the eleventh commandment in mind, "Thou shalt not fall," we were eager to move forward.

The Come to Jesus Meeting

Have you ever had a Come to Jesus meeting? Have you ever been faced with a difficult situation where you had to share honest words that others might perceive to be painful, unfair, or even unjust? I commended Rajiv for having the courage to speak honestly with his two clients because we were his responsibility, and all four of us were in this together, for better or worse. Rajiv was banking on his experience when making the decision to recommend turning back. However, past experience where trekkers could not handle the conditions does not always predict future scenarios. Each situation is unique and needs to be considered with grace as well as clarity.

What we were actually doing in our Come to Jesus meeting was employing the Rule of Christ that is laid out in Matthew 18. It should come as no surprise that the early church needed to develop procedures to address conflict resolution. Don't you just love differences? Differences are a part of the goodness of God's creation. Whether we like it or not, we live in an increasingly diverse and global world where most people do not look, talk, speak, dress, or worship like us.

Along with the necessity of interacting with people of different races, cultures, religions, languages, and countries comes the inevitable challenge of honoring, accepting, and even loving differences. Even the smallest of our towns and churches are no longer homogeneous. Our reality, however, is that the inability to understand and embrace differences as a gift from God can cause incredible heartache as well as bad behavior. God has created us as unique, one-of-a-kind individuals, gives us freedom, and puts us in community with one another. What a recipe for conflict, even in the church!

When we encounter a situation where we are not of one heart or mind with someone else, the first thing to do is look at ourselves and ask the questions, "How important are our differences on this issue? Can I let this go and chill out rather than make a big deal out of it? What does God see?" If you believe the issue is too important to simply forget about, turn to Matthew 18:15-20, which has been called the Rule of Christ for the Church.

> *"If your brother or sister sins against you, go and correct them when you are alone together. If they listen to you, then you've won over your brother or sister."*
>
> *(Matthew 18:15)*

Makes perfect sense, doesn't it? The person who has been harmed is the moral agent for transformation. But whom does that person usually speak to first? Why, everyone but the person who has hurt him or her! We want to garner support, so we talk to our friends, confide in the church secretary, send emails and tweets, spread it all over Facebook, and even, God forbid, call the district superintendent or write a letter to the bishop.

Matthew is writing his Gospel from the viewpoint of the needs of the early church. We're not sure what type of sins Matthew is referring to here, but they are clearly ones that threaten the unity of the body of Christ. In this verse, Jesus counsels church members to talk directly and privately to the person who has harmed them in order to avoid embarrassment and be sensitive to their feelings. That's how we best live together as family in the kingdom of God.

> *"But if they won't listen, take with you one or two others so that* every word may be established by the mouth of two or three witnesses.*"*
>
> *(Matthew 18:16)*

The role of witnesses is not to take sides but to be a mediating presence and to assist in the listening process. In a United Methodist church, either the chair or members, or both, of the Staff Parish Relations Committee (SPRC) might play this role if the pastor or a staff member is involved in a conflict with another staff or church member. If meeting with a mediator doesn't work, and reconciliation is not achieved, there is a third step.

"But if they still won't pay attention, report it to the church."
(Matthew 18:17a)

Evidently, the early Christian church had developed procedures for dealing with disputes, which could have involved an intervention of the group as a whole since the house churches were small. Today, this step might include a meeting with the pastor and the individuals involved, a meeting with the entire SPRC and a group that is upset, a meeting with the district superintendent and the parties involved, or the bringing in of a ministry consultant to facilitate reconciliation and healing in the congregation. Others who are not as patient might simply say, "Let's just move on."

"If they won't pay attention even to the church, treat them as you would a Gentile and tax collector. I assure you that whatever you fasten on earth will be fastened in heaven. And whatever you loosen on earth will be loosened in heaven. Again I assure you that if two of you agree on earth about anything you ask, then my Father who is in heaven will do it for you. For where two or three are gathered in my name, I'm there with them."
(Matthew 18:17b-20)

Verse 17b is the critical verse in the passage, and I would contend that how we interpret this verse depends on how we view God's work in the world. Most people see this verse as providing the earliest legal procedures for excommunication. Just as Gentiles and tax collectors were despised in their time, so we ought to turn our backs on those who sin until they repent.

Could it be that Jesus is thinking of something else here when he says, "Treat them as you would a Gentile and tax collector?" Since Jesus, in other scriptures, urges us to associate *with* tax collectors and spread the gospel *to* Gentiles, could Jesus be saying here that the person who has sinned should be the object of continuing love and missionary activity instead of shunning? Does the interpretation of excommunication reflect traditional prejudice against Gentiles and tax collectors from the conservative Jewish congregation to which Matthew is writing instead of reflecting the way of Jesus? Is this verse about judgment or grace?

How we interpret verse 17b depends on how we view God's work in our world. And don't forget: this scripture is framed by two other stories—the lost sheep before and the unforgiving servant after—both of which remind us that sinners are to be saved, not condemned. Eugene Peterson paraphrases verse 17 in *The Message*, "If he won't listen to the church, you'll have to start over from scratch, confront him with the need for repentance, and offer again God's forgiving love."

It's no coincidence that the scripture passage immediately following the Rule of Christ is about forgiveness. Forgiveness is an essential spiritual practice that transforms conflict, mends hearts, and heals lives. Without forgiveness, there is no reconciliation, no hope, and no health for us or our churches.

At the heart of healthy churches is conflict transformation. Hearts beat strong in local churches when we create a culture of loving differences and practicing open and honest communication. The most important aspect of resolving differences is careful and prayerful listening on everyone's part. My hope is that the church can model healthy ways of dialoguing about its own difficult issues so that we can be an example for how our world can manage its complex differences. Unfortunately, the church doesn't always do so well in this area, even in The United Methodist Church!

According to a national survey of congregations called Faith Communities Today,[10] the greatest predictor of church decline is destructive conflict. Conflict is a natural part of life. It's how we deal with conflict that's the problem. When humans are not able to deal constructively and creatively with conflict, we exhibit fear, anger, defensiveness, anxiety, and even violence.

What if you and I could learn to love differences? What if we could view our enemy as someone to help us see ourselves in a new way? What if conflict became an opportunity for spiritual growth—to grow healthy hearts and contribute to peace and justice in our world? Isn't it amazing that two thousand years ago, Jesus gave us practical wisdom for treating one another in healthy ways, maintaining church fellowship, and preserving the integrity of the community of faith?

We can pursue Jesus' wisdom by arranging Come to Jesus meetings and following these steps from Matthew 18:

- **We love differences and transform conflict by speaking the truth in love.** With humility, compassion, and respect for those with whom you disagree or who have harmed you, and knowing that God is there with you, will you dare to engage in direct, gentle, and holy conversation when you have a conflict with another person? And will you be open to where the wind of the Holy Spirit might take that conversation?

- **We love differences and transform conflict by letting go of self.** Conflict transformation is where God's work of love is done. It's where bad behaviors end, and new and healthy behaviors emerge. Conflict transformation recognizes that all people have been harmed and have harmed others. That includes you and me. This new way of being with others means letting go of our own misconceptions and desires and allowing ourselves to be vulnerable, fully present to God's grace, and open to change.

- **We love differences and transform conflict by seeing forgiveness as a choice and then a journey.** Forgiveness is grounded in the very nature of God, demanding great patience and mercy of ourselves and others. We can forgive with our minds, but our hearts often lag behind. Forgiveness does not mean tolerating bad behavior, however. Christians are often guilty of forgiving too much too quickly. As Alcoholics Anonymous reminds us, even in the midst of forgiveness there are consequences for bad behavior.

- **It is possible to love differences and transform conflict by learning how to apologize well when we have harmed others.** The steps to a good apology include listening to and understanding the story of the one we have harmed, confessing the hurt that has been caused, repenting by making things right, accepting accountability, and not harming again.

- **We love differences and transform conflict by creating a well, not a wall.** Tom Porter, former director of the Just-Peace Center for Mediation and Conflict transformation in The United Methodist Church, has used the image of a well to describe how we can bring others together, just as people the world over have gathered around wells for centuries to collect fresh, flowing water.[11] When we create wells and allow them to fill up with abundant, life-giving, healing water, then everyone can be well together.

Whether Rajiv knew it or not, he was following Jesus' instructions stating that when there is a problem with someone else, we need to go directly to that person and have an honest conversation rather than spread rumors or talk to others. That way we avoid embarrassing the other person and hurting his or her feelings. That's how we best live together in the kingdom of God. In this case, Rajiv spoke directly to me rather than triangulating my daughter, who was then welcomed into the conversation.

Through the spiritual discipline of listening and negotiation, we were able to move forward. In fact, for the rest of the trek, Rajiv, Talitha, and I were able to talk frankly and freely about how we felt, what effect the altitude had on us, and how the day had gone. Because there were just the four of us, we could personalize the trek in ways we could not with a larger group. I also believe we taught Rajiv a few things about stereotyping the abilities of women, whatever their age.

I believe that our greatest area of growth as United Methodist disciples of Jesus Christ is learning to speak with one another about difficult subjects. During thirty-eight years of active ministry, I have had countless Come to Jesus meetings, which never seem to get any easier with the passing years. However, I have become more comfortable, knowing that effective and fruitful ministry does not happen without learning how to have difficult conversations.

Why do we need Come to Jesus meetings? Because differences are a part of the goodness of God's creation. And because we are different, we have varied backgrounds, cultures, expectations, hopes, and dreams. Whether we like it or not, we live in an increasingly diverse and global world.

I learned early in my ministry to address hard issues head-on with transparency and grace because of a wise mentor who asked me to chair the personnel committee of a county hospice organization. I was a pastor in my early thirties and had never taken any classes in seminary related to supervision. My mentor, a physician, was a member of the United Methodist church where I was serving as an associate pastor, and he knew I needed to learn some new skills in order to grow in my ministry.

Through my mentor's gentle guidance, I was able to become a more capable supervisor. Over the years, as my ministry and leadership responsibilities have increased, Come to Jesus meetings have become more common. Although I still dread having the conversations, I also realize that I kind of enjoy negotiating and leading others through difficult issues. And I always experience grace and hope in the process.

Several Come to Jesus meetings stand out. One time I was working with a staff member who wanted to negotiate flexible hours by working at odd times when no other staff members were present. I was sympathetic to the staff member's need to accommodate family. However, my efforts to be helpful made life very difficult for other staff members with whom this person needed to work but who were not available in the wee hours of the morning. Finally, a few staff members initiated a Come to Jesus meeting with me, pointing out that my desire to help the person who needed flexibility was raising other issues that were far more significant and would impede the ministries of a number of other people. In other words, I was being too gracious. I finally listened and made the right decision.

In another setting, the chair of the Staff Parish Relations Committee and I agreed that we needed to have a Come to Jesus meeting with a staff member whose personal issues were getting in the way of that person's effectiveness. Unfortunately, by the time the meeting took place, this person was so debilitated that things did not go well. We ended up doing the right thing by asking the person to resign, but it was probably not the right time or place or setting to have that meeting. I keep humbly moving on toward perfection, always praying for God's grace to lead me.

Come to Jesus conversations are very difficult to have in churches, whether it is around either declining church attendance or finances, or both; interpersonal difficulties; or issues with staff or the pastor. At the same time, learning how to have difficult but respectful, grace-filled, and honest conversations when there are issues is a necessary and critical skill for leaders in the church today. We are also called to model for the world how to be with one another and negotiate in good faith.

Tips for Come to Jesus Meetings

One of the most necessary skills for clergy and other professionals who supervise others is negotiating though conflict.

If you are the leader, keep in mind the following points:

1. Take the initiative to arrange the Come to Jesus meeting. Don't avoid it because the conflict won't go away. It will likely just get worse.
2. Pray for grace.
3. Invite the person with whom you are meeting to bring a support person.
4. Show respect, gentleness, and kindness toward the person with whom you need to have a difficult conversation.
5. Remember the times when you have been in their shoes.
6. Listen carefully before speaking.
7. Go into the meeting with eyes and hearts open to possibly being wrong.
8. Be transparent and honest.
9. Know that Jesus is present.
10. Keeping the peace will not solve the problem.

If you are the focus of someone else's criticism, try to remember the following points:

1. Do not be defensive.
2. Show grace to those who are accusing you.
3. Be willing to listen to what may be hard words to hear.
4. If you are wrong, admit it with humility.
5. Take responsibility if you goof.
6. Don't make assumptions about the other person.
7. Ask to bring a support person.
8. Be transparent.
9. If you believe you have been misinterpreted, be direct and nonanxious.
10. Know that God is with you.

I applaud our guide for addressing what he perceived to be a potential hazard and danger if I was not able to complete what, admittedly, was a very challenging trek. In hindsight, Rajiv may have exaggerated the difficulty of the rest of the trip because it was not as muddy and slippery as the first two days. However, we were able to talk openly, and I could reassure him that I was physically able to complete the trek. In the end, building authentic relationships always breaks down barriers.

Rajiv, Bishal, Talitha, and I could have experienced a pretty miserable trek if we had not had that Come to Jesus meeting. I am glad that Rajiv was willing to have honest conversation. But, most of all, I'm glad that the four of us decided together to keep on keeping on with anticipation and grace.

Chapter
3

Unlike so much of life around the world, the bread of life is offered to all people without charge. It's free. We just need to accept God's grace, which, in turn, prompts us to live for Jesus.

Chapter 3
You Must Eat More!

We always woke up on the trail before 6 a.m. because starting out before it became too hot was a priority. What a difference a day made! The extreme mud and slipperiness of the first several days dissipated as we moved to higher elevations. Unfortunately, it wasn't the most restful night because of some intestinal issues. Plus, there was a tarantula in the bathroom, which was an all-too-common occurrence.

After packing up all our stuff, it was time for coffee and breakfast. I have never been a coffee drinker, but Rajiv, Bishal, and Talitha always started their day with a cup of joe. Traditionally, Nepalis have been tea drinkers rather than coffee drinkers, and tea continues to be the favorite national drink, with tea stalls found everywhere in the larger towns and cities. Even though coffee has been considered the drink of tourists, it has become much more popular everywhere in Nepal over the last decade or so. Not so with me!

Daily life on the trail revolved around food for two good reasons. First, each one of us expended an enormous number of calories trekking for much of the day. And, second, the trails are not like the nice walking paths that we find in many communities in the United States. Not one of the trails we traveled was paved, there was no signage whatsoever, and virtually every trail demanded complete attention on our part in order to avoid falling.

As a long-distance runner, I am aware that the daily energy and endurance we need comes from good nutrition. Breakfast, especially, needs to contain protein, which is critical for developing and maintaining lean muscle. Americans consume lots of protein, but most of it is at the evening meal. When we do not eat enough protein during the day, however, our muscles are not maintained at their maximum level. In addition, eating protein at breakfast has kept us feeling full longer and helps us avoid between-meal snacking. For the past twenty years, my breakfast of cottage cheese and fruit, especially grapes and blueberries, keeps my energy level high during the morning.

The challenge in Nepal was that the food available for breakfast was different from the food we eat every day at home. The first day on the trail we had porridge, which did not keep me filled up until lunch. Although the oats in porridge contain some protein, we just didn't eat enough in relation to the calories we expended.

One morning we had what looked and tasted like an elephant ear with honey. It probably didn't give us the protein with which we needed to start the day, and Talitha and I both felt sluggish. We were working hard and needed substance. At the same time, we experienced firsthand how people who are poor and do not have enough protein suffer physically as well as mentally.

The staple meal in the remote area of Nepal in which we were trekking is *dal bhat*, which consists of lentil soup, boiled rice, and curried vegetables. If Nepal had a national dish, this would be it. Occasionally, side dishes—such as cooked vegetables, pickles, meat or fish, yogurt, and chutney—are added when available. Rajiv and Bishal often ate dal bhat for both lunch and dinner. As we trekked higher into the Himalayas, potatoes and *tsampa*—which is roasted flour—usually from barley, became more prevalent.

Variety in foods is quite limited in the isolated villages of the Himalayas where there are no grocery stores around the corner. Villagers eat what they can raise themselves on steep mountainside terraces. The most common foods are rice, lentils, eggs, and vegetables, with meat not always available. Everything is fresh, and if you can't grow it yourself, you can't afford to eat it. In the poorest countries of the world, food is pared down to its most basic components. We knew that the people in the villages where we stayed ate similar food, and I was continually praying for their health and welfare.

When we took breaks during the day, we had to eat. We focused on protein bars from home, knowing that we would not receive all the nutrition we needed from our meals. Rajiv kept reminding us, "You must eat more!" Unfortunately, I could not eat two big bowls of porridge or dal bhat like Rajiv and Bishal could. And I confess that I felt like a spoiled American because I found it a challenge to eat the same thing at every meal. Intense physical exertion demanded more food, but my body was definitely burning more calories than I was consuming.

I was not sure what might happen after last night's Come to Jesus meeting. However, after the first hour of slogging through the mud and slippery rocks, today's trek ended up being much better than the first two days. The scenery was gorgeous, we were climbing, and the steps were not as steep and were, for the most part, dry. Plus, we walked through some beautiful villages. Rajiv said that we were ahead of schedule.

All of the rooms in which we stayed overnight were basic, and most had no electricity. The early darkness made doing the most routine things in our room challenging, but we still had fun. Talitha and I both had iPads and spent the evenings reading in our sleeping bags. Dinner was different on our fourth night. We had a Tibetan dish called *momos*: eggs and veggies in a dumpling-like cover. They were delicious!

Talitha and I had been going around and around about water and had been paying for bottled water so far. However, the price of water started to increase the higher we trekked into remote high mountain areas. We decide to experiment that day with water purification and iodine tablets, which worked well.

Every day, as we trekked, we experienced grace upon grace, with many new experiences. Eventually, eggs became available for the first time, so I would have a hard-boiled egg and ciabatta bread for breakfast. We covered a variety of terrain in the initial days of the trek, the most interesting being a new temporary trail skirting around a landslide that happened a few days before. In addition, three times during the trek, I encountered a Nepali child or adult who was also wearing a splint on an arm. Sharing a common bond, we would both raise our incapacitated arms and smile.

As we occasionally passed small villages along the trail, we made a point to connect with the children, all of whom knew some basic English. We enjoyed watching them play. Soccer and volleyball were especially popular for the teenagers. What the children asked for the most was chocolate. Sadly, we could not carry chocolate with us because it would quickly melt on warm days.

Almost all of the villages we passed through did not have ready access to the outside world. There were no roads or cars, so villagers needed to be self-sufficient. Most of the families were farmers. Every day we observed numerous helicopters fly through the area, bringing medical help for emergencies and supplies not otherwise available for the residents.

Wanting to know more about this gorgeous country with such beautiful people, I came across The Borgen Project, which is a nonprofit organization formed in Seattle in 2003 in order to fight extreme global poverty around the world. In 2018 The Borgen Project updated its list of ten facts about poverty in Nepal, a country of 30 million people.[12]

I learned that Nepal, a nation of 30 million people, has witnessed over seventy civil wars since 1945. This civil unrest has contributed to the fact that five million Nepalese are malnourished and living in extreme poverty. Other factors include lack of health care, education, and jobs, rising food and housing prices, high child mortality rates, corruption in government, mountainous geography, and limited farming methods.

At the same time, Habitat for Humanity is active in Nepal. According to The Borgen Project, Habitat is building 2.3 houses per hour in the country. The efforts of Habitat, other nonprofit organizations, and many volunteers are making a positive difference in the quality of life in Nepal.

I had been working very hard physically and had been able to keep up so far without broken bones or falls! The trekking had stretched me in every way possible. One afternoon we even spent a few dollars for a bucket of hot water in lieu of another cold shower. We had been enjoying momos for dinner the past few days, but still we were hungry. I fantasized about what it would be like to eat a hamburger. Meanwhile, Rajiv kept urging us to eat more, knowing that the more energy we expended climbing, the more calories we needed.

Many people in the US eat way too much because whatever we want is literally in front of us all the time. The amount of food that is wasted in America is obscene. Here, it is just the opposite because the variety of food is limited, and nothing goes to waste. I ended up losing eight pounds in twelve days, simply because I was working so hard and not eating enough. I also caught a glimpse of the poverty and malnutrition of much of the world.

After dinner one night high in the Himalayas, Rajiv, Talitha, and I stayed in the small restaurant because it had electricity and light, and we tentatively plotted out the rest of the trip by looking at the map. I wondered why there were five other groups of people sitting around tables in this very remote mountain village, when a sense of wonder came over me. This was the night of the finals of the World Cup in Moscow with France versus Croatia. In this practically inaccessible location, people were gathered around a TV in the bar! How stunningly strange it was to be sitting in a tiny restaurant in rural, mountainous Nepal, united together by soccer.

Jesus as the Bread of Life

Jesus said to them, "I am the bread of life. Whoever comes to me will never be hungry, and whoever believes in me will never be thirsty." . . .

Then the Jews began to complain about him because he said, "I am the bread that came down from heaven." They were saying, "Is not this Jesus, the son of Joseph, whose father and mother we know? How can he now say, 'I have come down from heaven'?" . . . [Jesus said,] "I am the living bread that came down from heaven. Whoever eats of this bread will live forever; and the bread that I will give for the life of the world is my flesh."

The Jews then disputed among themselves, saying, "How can this man give us his flesh to eat?" So Jesus said to them, "Very truly, I tell you, unless you eat the flesh of the Son of Man and drink his blood, you have no life in you. . . . This is the bread that came down from heaven, not like that which your ancestors ate, and they died. But the one who eats this bread will live forever." He said these things while he was teaching in the synagogue at Capernaum.

When many of his disciples heard it, they said, "This teaching is difficult; who can accept it?" But Jesus, being aware that his disciples were complaining about it, said to them, "Does this offend you? Then what if you were to see the Son of Man ascending to where he was before? It is the spirit that gives life; the flesh is useless. The words that I have spoken to you are spirit and life."

(John 6:35, 41-42, 51-53, 58-63 NRSV)

It's the evening of the day that Jesus feeds the five thousand. After Jesus realizes that the people wish to make him king, he withdraws to the mountain by himself. In the evening, the disciples get into a boat and start across the Sea of Galilee to Capernaum. "A strong wind was blowing and the waters grew rough" (John 6: 18 NIV), but they row about three or four miles. Meanwhile, Jesus starts walking on the sea and comes near the boat. He says, "It is I. Don't be afraid" (verse 20 NIV). The disciples want to take Jesus with them in the boat, but just then, they reach their destination.

The next day the crowd cannot find Jesus, so they get into boats and go to Capernaum and ask Jesus, "How did you get here?" Jesus replies, "I know what you're after. I fed you. Are you interested in me as the source of bread or as the Son of God? Don't work for food that perishes but for food that endures for eternal life, which the Son of Man will give you. Truly I tell you, it wasn't Moses who gave you bread from heaven. It is my Father who gives you the true bread from heaven. I am the bread of life. Whoever comes to me will never be hungry, and whoever believes in me will never be thirsty. Whoever eats my bread will live forever, and the bread that I give to the world is my flesh. You don't need a sign. I am the sign."

Bread is called the staff of life because it's a very basic form of sustenance that supports human existence. Some form of bread is found in every society. The variety is endless, just like the variety of people on this earth. Tea bread, challah bread, rye bread, whole grain bread, dinner rolls, English muffins, banana bread, sourdough bread, bagels, gluten-free bread, ciabatta bread, French toast, and roti. Roti is Nepali flat bread made from the wheat flour, traditionally known as *atta*.[13]

Notice, Jesus doesn't say, "I am caviar. I am filet mignon or crème brûlée or asparagus or lobster." No, Jesus says, "I am the bread of life. I am accessible to everyone, for whoever comes to me will never be hungry and whoever believes in me will never be thirsty." Then the Jews in Capernaum begin to complain. "Wait just a minute. Isn't this Joseph's son who is saying this? How can Jesus say he is bread come down from heaven? Besides that, how can Jesus say he is giving us his flesh to eat?" Jesus replies, "Very truly I tell you, unless you eat the flesh of the Son of Man and drink his blood, you have no life in you. The one who eats this bread will live forever."

Jesus' disciples are also in Capernaum, and when they hear Jesus' words, they, too, are taken aback. "Wow! This teaching is difficult. Who can accept it?" And Jesus, overhearing them and aware that they're complaining, too, says, "Does this offend you? The words I have spoken to you are spirit and life."

Could it be that in proclaiming himself to be the bread of life Jesus is not only inviting his followers but invites you and me to reshape our own attitudes and spiritual practices? Why is this such a difficult teaching? And why would it have been offensive to his disciples as well as to others who heard Jesus?

A Conflict over Bread

First, this is a difficult saying because many of us seek a different kind of bread. The Jews want signs that Jesus is the Son of God. They want more miracles. They want proof. Just like the manna that magically came down from heaven to feed the Israelites, they want even more spectacular miracles. But Jesus says, "You're looking for the wrong kind of bread. I am bread. What gives life is not physical bread. Nor is it money, success, status, or appearance. What gives life is my body and blood, given for you. Follow me, and you will experience true life."

Do you know that some people today are offended by bread? Yes, they are! We twenty-first-century Americans seem to have a love/hate relationship with bread because of the dreaded word *carbohydrates*. Many people today don't even eat bread at home or in restaurants because it contains too many carbs. We're told that if we diet, we need to forsake bread and anything with flour, especially white flour.

In her 2015 book, *Wearing God*, best-selling Christian author Lauren Winner cites a study of women with eating disorders. Two-thirds of the women said that they decrease the frequency of receiving Communion because they are afraid of the calories in the bread and the juice.[14] What does this say about a society where we are obsessed with food, where we both idolize and demonize food, and where we are ashamed of our relationship with food? What does it mean to say that Jesus is the bread of life when we are conflicted about our own attitudes toward food and appearance?

The same year, 2015, Mattel came out with a new line of Barbie dolls after fifty years of an ultrathin Barbie physique that is unattainable for 99.9 percent of girls. Mattel unveiled the Fashionistas line featuring Barbies of many different ethnicities. Then, in 2016, "Mattel introduced three new body shapes for Barbie in an attempt to make her look more realistic: curvy, tall, and petite."[15] And in February 2019, Mattel announced that the Fashionistas line would add two dolls with disabilities by June 2019. One Barbie comes with a wheelchair, and another Barbie has a removable prosthetic leg.

In many ways, you and I live in the land of the feast of death. Out there is the table of eternal hunger where bread is called money. Yet in the midst of the feast of death sits the table of the Lord. Our hunger is satisfied here. When we place our whole trust in Jesus and lay our very lives at his feet, our souls are nourished unto eternal life.

A Freely Offered Bread

There's a second reason why this teaching is offensive. It's offensive because the bread of life is offered to all people, free of charge. There is nothing we can do to deserve the bread of life or prevent others from having it. Yet this is diametrically opposed to the slang definition of "bread" as "money." As Talitha, Rajiv, Bishal, and I sat in the tiny restaurant high in the Himalayan Mountains of Nepal, I wondered about all of the bread (money) that was changing hands at the World Cup soccer championship that night. Unlike so much of life around the world, the bread of life is offered to all people without charge. It's free. We just need to accept God's grace, which, in turn, prompts us to live for Jesus.

A Life-Changing Bread

A third reason why Jesus' words are offensive is because not only does Jesus tell us that true life is found in someone who gave up his life for others, but he also says that you and I find true life when we, too, become humble servants who lose our lives in serving all people in our world with love and grace.

The Jews believed that salvation could be attained through works. If they just followed the law, they would be fine. But Jesus came into the world to gently remind us that we're not capable of following the law. We can't ever get right with God by doing good things. Rather, Jesus offered his flesh and blood on a cross in order to set us right. Jesus did for us what we cannot do for ourselves. Jesus gave us his life out of love. His death was pure grace, an undeserved gift.

Now that's great news for those of us who are aware of our sins and know our need for grace. But it's offensive to those who always do the right thing and have no need of God's grace. It's a difficult concept to believe that salvation comes simply through accepting the bread Jesus offers.

Imagine how the Jews would have heard Jesus. To accept Jesus' words that he is the bread of life essentially would cut them off from their Jewish heritage and from everything that gave them identity and security: circumcision, keeping the law, making sacrifices, dietary restrictions. More than that, believing in Jesus meant that now the Jews were no longer God's only chosen people. Now anyone who believed could receive the bread of life!

The scandal is that no one can earn the bread of life. And no one deserves the bread of life. Not even we Americans, who, since our beginning, have placed so much value on pulling ourselves up by our own bootstraps, and, at the same time, keeping score of everyone else's missteps. The scandal is that the bread is free. Pure grace. In the words of Robert Farrar Capon, "Grace cannot prevail until our lifelong certainty that someone is keeping score has run out of steam and collapsed."[16] Like yeast, grace permeates the bread of life.

Does this offend you? Is this teaching difficult? Oh, yes, it is. Because of it, John says that many turned away and left Jesus.

So, Jesus asks his disciples, "Do you also wish to go away?" And Peter answered, "Lord, to whom can we go? You have the words of eternal life" (John 6:67-68 NRSV).

The challenge is that many of us think being a servant is an obligation rather than a privilege. It's a burden rather than a joy. It's oppression rather than liberation. But the truth is that when we are nourished by the bread of life, we not only receive strength for the journey, but we discover that by reaching out to the least, the last, and the lost and becoming their companions on the journey, we find true meaning, hope, and joy.

Do you know where the word *companion* comes from? The English word *companion* comes from two Latin words, *com*, which means "with," and *panis*, which means "bread."[17] A companion, then, is someone with whom we share our bread.

Most of us prefer to eat with people who are like us. And we tend to judge others by those with whom they eat and invite to their table. Critics of Jesus repeatedly pointed out that he dined with sinners, women, prostitutes, the poor, despised, outcasts, and sinners. But what Jesus is saying by eating with those whom others reject is this: "These are my companions. These also are children of God."

The bread of life is meant to break down walls and dispense grace because there is no difference between them and us, right? But it was offensive, and you know where it ultimately led Jesus? To the cross. Do you see any commercials for crosses at the World Cup or the Super Bowl?

At the same time that the bread of life offers grace and hope to all, many of us struggle to live whole and healthy lives, not only in Nepal but around the world and even in the United States. On April 25, 2019, Gallup released its Gallup 2019 Global Emotions Report.[18] In 2018 Gallup conducted 151,000 interviews with adults in over 140 countries to measure their emotional well-being. The adults were asked to describe both their positive and negative experiences the previous day. This annual poll was started in 2005.

The Global Emotions Report detailed the results of their findings, which indicated that 71 percent of people worldwide experienced a lot of enjoyment the day before the survey. Paraguay had the highest positive index score worldwide at 85, and Afghanistan's positive index score dropped to a record low 43.

The poll also showed that Americans registered their highest levels of stress and worry in over a decade. Julie Ray, Gallup's managing editor for world news, told *The New York Times*, "What really stood out for the U.S. is the increase in the negative experiences. This was kind of a surprise to us when we saw the numbers head in this direction."[19]

According to the *Times* article on the Global Emotional Report,

> In the United States, about 55 percent of adults said they had experienced stress during "a lot of the day" prior, compared with just 35 percent globally. Statistically, that put the country on par with Greece, which had led the rankings on stress since 2012.
>
> About 45 percent of the Americans surveyed said they had felt "a lot" of worry the day before, compared with a global average of 39 percent. Meanwhile, the share of Americans who reported feeling "a lot" of anger the day before being interviewed was the same as the global average: 22 percent.[20]

It is clear that people the world over experience a mixture of positive and negative emotions. While stress and anger can often be traced to global issues such as poverty, violence, worry, racism, oppression, and hunger, the report also shows that even people who seem to have everything they need also experience negative emotions that mitigate against enjoying the fullness of life that Jesus freely offers to all. At the same time, many people who have very little and live simply off the land, including much of the country of Nepal, are able to live well and experience happiness.

I love bread. I suspect you do as well. So did Jesus. That's why he said to his followers, "I am the bread of life. . . . The one who eats this bread will live forever." May God give us grace to seek the sustenance of both physical and spiritual bread, offer it to all who hunger, and invite them to be our companions on the journey.

Chapter
4

*As I kept thinking about the incident,
I began to ponder the nature of loss.
It was just a backpack, after all. At the same
time, my backpack contained everything
that was essential to trekking in Nepal. . . .
I wondered, "Is God trying to teach me
something important?"*

Chapter 4

It's Just a Backpack

Pumpkin soup again for breakfast wasn't exactly what my body craved. I know that I did not eat enough, but, thankfully, we were not trekking as far today as in other days. It was hard going, though, and we were steadily gaining elevation.

After an hour, we stopped to catch our breath and eat a protein bar. We were traversing a narrow path along the edge of a cliff and could see the Budhi Gandaki River far below, winding its way through a canyon.

I left my backpack at the edge of the path as I walked into the bush to take a bathroom break. It was a relief to be free of my backpack for a few minutes because the last few days I'd had issues with my pack not resting properly on the back of my neck, causing increasing discomfort.

Unfortunately, I left my backpack sitting on the wrong side of the trail. As I was walking away, I heard a whoosh! Looking back in horror, I saw my backpack disappear over the edge of the cliff. The valley was many thousands of feet below. If my pack moved even a few inches, I would lose it forever.

I frantically yelled for Rajiv to come, then leaned over and saw that my backpack was miraculously perched on top of a group of branches. I heaved a sigh of relief but knew we weren't out of the woods yet.

Rajiv was greatly concerned and completely focused. First, he tried using a trekking pole to grab the backpack handle, but it didn't work. We were afraid one wrong movement might push my pack through the branches into the void. Then Rajiv daringly lay on the ground and edged himself over the cliff.

Without warning, we had come to a moment of crisis in our trek. We literally held our breath as Bishal held Rajiv's ankles and slowly lowered him down. To our amazement, Rajiv was able to stretch out his hand and retrieve the backpack. Just as incredible was the faith and trust that Rajiv had in Bishal! Bishal literally held Rajiv's life in his hands.

Rajiv turned and walked away for a few minutes to gather himself together and lower his heart rate. When he returned, we all started moving again, but no one talked. When the time was right, I apologized profusely to Rajiv and promised never to do such a foolish thing again. One of the cardinal rules of trekking is never, never, ever lay your backpack on the cliff side of the trail. I felt convicted. Was my backpack worth Rajiv's risking his life?

Later that day, I asked Rajiv if something like this had ever happened to him before. He said no. I guess that means Rajiv will never forget this particular trekking adventure. Nor will I. For most of the day, I was quiet, staying within myself and considering the fact that this trek was difficult enough without making thoughtless mistakes.

As I kept thinking about the incident, I began to ponder the nature of loss. It was just a backpack, after all. At the same time, my backpack contained everything that was essential to trekking in Nepal: namely, my passport, visa, credit cards, cash, and prescriptions, especially Diamox for altitude sickness. But there was also my iPad, journal, toiletries, and what few clothes I brought with me.

I wondered, "Is God trying to teach me something important?" I suspect it was simply that I should always pay attention and not do it again. But there was more to it. If my backpack had tumbled through the branches into the abyss, it would have been a great loss. A game changer, to be sure. We would likely have had to end the trek, find our way back to civilization, and obtain another passport so I could get home.

Thinking back to how many times people I know, including me, have lost something and made a big deal out of it, I would always say, "Don't worry. It's just a phone (or a book, or a jacket, or a pair of shoes). You can always get another one. Things can be replaced, but you only have one life."

As a child, I led a fairly sheltered life and never had to deal with loss, other than the death of family dogs and cats. My paternal grandfather died before I was born, and my maternal grandfather died when I was about five. I have only vague memories of him.

My first great loss changed the course of my life. When I was in ninth grade, our growing Mennonite church built a beautiful but simple new building on the outskirts of our small town of Souderton in southeastern Pennsylvania. We also commissioned a free-standing tracker action pipe organ by C. B. Fisk, Inc., that became very well known in the area.

In tenth grade, I attended an organ recital given by the daughter of our associate pastor at the time. Her name was Joan Keller, and this was her senior organ recital for college. I remember vividly how magnificent her organ playing was and how gorgeous the instrument itself sounded. I love music and remember thinking, "Maybe I could learn how to play the organ, too." Not too long after the recital, Joan was tragically killed in a car accident on the campus of her college, right before her graduation.

Joan's death devastated me because she had become my hero. I had no idea how to cope with my own loss, let alone sympathize with the debilitating grief experienced by Joan's parents, especially her father, Pastor Frank, who was my youth group director. Several months later, I asked my father if I could take organ lessons. This began a period of ten years where the organ was at the center of my life until I felt a call to pastoral ministry.

I was so enamored with the organ that during my last two years of high school, I would wake up at 5:30 a.m. in the dark and drive to the church, where I had my own key to unlock the front door, and practice in a sanctuary inhabited only by the presence of the Holy Spirit. Twelve years later, it was Rev. Frank Keller, by then serving as a regional minister in Kansas, who ordained me in the General Conference Mennonite Church.

Loss became much more real to me when I became a pastor. My very first funeral was for a teenage boy from the first church I served in northern lower Michigan. John died in a one-car crash in the middle of the night on his way home. This was also my first experience of being awakened by the police in the wee hours of the morning and sent out to the house of a soon-to-be grieving family. In this case, I was already close to this young man's parents.

I have vivid memories of sitting with John's parents as the police informed them of their son's death. In fact, this couple had taken a special liking to our first child, who was born several weeks after we arrived at the church in the summer of 1981. They were surrogate grandparents for our young daughter. The academic preparation of seminary could not adequately prepare me to walk me through the incredible grief that this precious family experienced.

With each succeeding loss in my ministry career, I learned more about life and death and about distancing myself enough from the pain to minister with tenderness and grace. I had to keep my own feelings in check as I drove to the hospital to sit with the body of another teenager who had just drowned in a local lake and then sit with his mother through most of the night.

Walking with a young couple through the cancer diagnosis and death of a baby was an unfathomable and virtually unbearable loss. In the same way, seeing a young adult struggle with a terminal disease with courage and deep faith gave me hope. One woman put it very well as we stood in the narthex before the funeral for her beloved husband, "At a time like this, I don't know how I can feel such sadness . . . and such joy."

Learning to live with loss changes our perspective on life and makes us stronger and more compassionate. That's why I was able to let go that day high in the Himalayas and say, "It's just a backpack." Everything in perspective. Most important is knowing that God walks with us no matter what. Romans 14:8 came to mind, "If we live, we live for the Lord, and if we die, we die for the Lord. Therefore, whether we live or die, we belong to God."

We reached our destination early in the afternoon so that we would have time to acclimate to the higher elevation. We could already feel the change in altitude and the colder weather. After resting for a while, Rajiv took us on a twenty-five-minute walk up the mountain, which wasn't as bad as it could have been because we left our backpacks in our rooms. Rajiv's goal was twofold: to help us acclimate further to the higher altitude and also to visit a school for boys and a Buddhist monastery where fifteen monks lived.

According to *The World Factbook*, produced by the Central Intelligence Agency, the following religions are practiced in Nepal (2011 estimation): 81.3 percent of the population of Nepal is Hindu, 9 percent is Buddhist, 4.4 percent is Muslim, 3.1 percent is Kirant (indigenous ethnic religion), 1.4 percent is Christian, 0.5 percent is other, and 0.2 percent are followers of unspecified faiths.[21] In the area of our trek, our experience was primarily with Buddhism.

As we entered the Buddhist temple, we took off our shoes and Rajiv explained the various paintings and important pictures of people, including the Lama, which is a title for a teacher of the Dharma, or teaching, in Tibetan Buddhism. Having had little exposure to Buddhism, my attention was completely focused on observing, learning, and letting go of all preconceived notions.

Although Christianity and Buddhism are very different, they do hold one important concept in common. Both religions emphasize the pattern of death and resurrection. In Matthew 16:25, we read, "All who want to save their lives will lose them. But all who lose their lives because of me will find them."

Death and life are part of the same process. In order to find true life, we must surrender our desires, our wants, and our very selves. By dying to self, we discover new life in a deeper way, which is a common pattern in nature. Buddha, Hindu gurus, Muhammad, and Jesus all saw this pattern in history: a necessary suffering and even dying so that something new can emerge.

The most important architectural form for Buddhists is the *stupa*, a stepped pyramid that is a ceremonial burial mound used for the veneration of Buddhist saints and relics. We passed many stupas, high up in the Himalayas, during the course of our trek.

Siddhartha Gautama, who was the historical Buddha, died in the fifth century BCE. During that time, burial mounds were built to inter kings and other important people. After the Buddha's death, his cremated remains were divided into eight parts and interred in stupas in each one of the eight kingdoms where the Buddha had lived.

Today, stupas dot the mountains of Nepal. They serve as a reminder of the teaching of Buddhism and as a gathering place for meditation and discussion.

Buddhists visit stupas to perform rituals that help them to achieve one of the most important goals of Buddhism: to understand the Buddha's teachings, known as the Four Noble Truths. Those truths are:

- Suffering exists.
- Suffering is caused by desire (and ignorance).
- It is possible to end suffering.
- The end to suffering may be achieved by following the Noble Eightfold Path, a set of resolutions characterized by right knowledge, right aspiration, right speech, right conduct, right means of livelihood, right endeavour, right mindfulness, and right meditation.[22]

Rajiv emphasized that it is important to walk around stupas clockwise so that the walls of the stupa are on the right side. To walk counter-clockwise is considered a sign of disrespect. On our way back to our teahouse, a group of elderly Nepalese was sitting on the ground, chanting Buddhist prayers. Buddhists do not pray to a God like Christians do, but they do observe devotional meditational practices that are similar to prayer, such as radiating loving-kindness to all human beings. They gave us permission to take their picture.

We'd now had two short days in a row, meant to further acclimate ourselves to the altitude and also preserve our energy for the big day when we were to leave at 3:30 a.m. to crest the Larkya Pass. In the afternoon, Rajiv offered to take us up to a beautiful lake about forty-five minutes away by foot. It was raining, however, so we chose to stay in our sleeping bags, take a nap, and read. We were also hoping that the clothes that we hand-washed a few days ago might finally have had a chance to dry.

Later in the day, Talitha and I took a stroll through the muddy streets of Sando to purchase a few Snickers bars and some cookies for the several tough days ahead when we crested the pass. The farther up we climbed, the colder it was. I was finding it difficult to stay warm at night, even when I was wearing all of my clothes in my sleeping bag. I took to filling my water bottle with boiling hot water and sticking it inside my sleeping bag so that I didn't freeze.

One day at a time, I kept reminding myself. Just as we couldn't rush up the mountain but had to follow the proper protocol in order to acclimate to the altitude, so Jesus reminds us to engage each day to the fullest, surrendering what we do not yet know or cannot change, and leaving tomorrow up to God.

Not to Worry

"No one can serve two masters. Either you will hate the one and love the other, or you will be loyal to the one and have contempt for the other. You cannot serve God and wealth.

"Therefore, I say to you, don't worry about your life, what you'll eat or what you'll drink, or about your body, what you'll wear. Isn't life more than food and the body more than clothes? Look at the birds in the sky. They don't sow seed or harvest grain or gather crops into barns. Yet your heavenly Father feeds them. Aren't you worth much more than they are? Who among you by worrying can add a single moment to your life? And why do you worry about clothes? Notice how the lilies in the field grow. They don't wear themselves out with work, and they don't spin cloth. But I say to you that even Solomon in all of his splendor wasn't dressed like one of these. If God dresses grass in the field so beautifully, even though it's alive today and tomorrow it's thrown into the furnace, won't God do much more for you, you people of weak faith? Therefore, don't worry and say, 'What are we going to eat?' or 'What are we going to drink?' or 'What are

we going to wear?' Gentiles long for all these things. Your
heavenly Father knows that you need them. Instead, desire
first and foremost God's kingdom and God's righteousness,
and all these things will be given to you as well. Therefore,
stop worrying about tomorrow, because tomorrow will worry
about itself. Each day has enough trouble of its own."
(Matthew 6:24–34)

According to a 1966 issue of the *Langholm Old Church Parish Magazine*,[23] in April 1913, a world-renowned physician stood up to address the medical students at Yale University. His name was Sir William Osler, and, at the time, he was the Regius Professor of Medicine at Oxford. Not only was Osler the author of the greatest standard medical textbook of his day, but by his teaching and example, "he had raised the practice of medicine on two continents to a new level of dignity and service."

In addition to being a brilliant medical mind, Sir William Osler was also a lover of English literature and a highly respected philosopher. Besides all of that, Osler was an intensely human person, a warm gregarious personality, full of fun. He was happy, radiant, zestful, keenly interested in people, never forgetting a name or a face, and finding his chief delight in playing with little children and writing letters to them.

Think about that: a world-famous physician, author, and lecturer, one of the most eminent men of science in his day, taking time to write letters to little children. How could any one person crowd into a single day such a wide range of activities contributing so much to his profession and to the world, and yet still find ample time to play and read, to think and study, to love and rest and celebrate life so vibrantly? Sir William Osler had a secret. He called it his "philosophy of life," and it was this philosophy that he shared with the students at Yale University that day.

It was the practice of living one day at a time. Osler called it living "in day-tight-compartments," the parish magazine stated. He said, "Throw away all ambition beyond that of doing the day's work well. The travellers on the road to success live in the present, heedless of taking thought for the morrow. Live neither in the past nor in the future, but let each day's work absorb your entire energies and satisfy your widest ambition."

Yet, we are a nation of worriers. I suspect that Americans worry more than any other people on this earth. We worry about our children, our parents, our jobs, our marriages, our churches, our schools, our nation, the economy, our health care, and our world. We are stressed-out folks. All we need to do is watch the commercials during the evening news. What is advertised? All sorts of remedies for upset stomachs, headaches, ulcers, hypertension, hemorrhoids, insomnia, anxiety, and sexual dysfunction, all of which can be products of too much worry.

I confess that I am no different than anyone else in that I am often consumed with worry. I frequently wake up in the morning with a pit in my stomach because I am anxious about the enormity of my responsibilities and the lives that will be affected by the decisions I have to make.

In contrast to all of this, Jesus tells us very simply not to worry about our lives or what we will eat or drink or wear. Why? Because if God can care for the birds of the air and the lilies of the field, how much more will God care for you? Besides, there is something much more important than worry. "Instead, desire first and foremost God's kingdom and God's righteousness," Jesus says, "and all these things will be given to you as well. Therefore, stop worrying about tomorrow, because tomorrow will worry about itself. Each day has enough trouble of its own" (Matthew 6:33-34).

This scripture is part of Jesus' Sermon on the Mount, which is his first public teaching in the Gospel of Matthew. The Sermon on the Mount provides a snapshot of what a righteous life looks like and why we cannot enter the kingdom of heaven without letting go of all that separates us from God. This particular passage about worry comes right on the heels of Jesus' saying that we cannot serve two masters at the same time: God and wealth.

The creative tension of all of Jesus' teachings is that his standards of righteousness are so high that we assume we cannot possibly attain them. Can anyone live a just, righteous, and holy life where we never worry, hate our enemies, judge others, get angry, or neglect the poor and the needy? Of course not. The apostle Paul is clear about the paradoxical nature of the Christian life when he laments, "I don't know what I'm doing, because I don't do what I want to do. Instead, I do the thing that I hate" (Romans 7:15). Paul discovered that he could not be righteous through the Jewish law but only by the grace of Jesus Christ and the power of the Holy Spirit.

Jesus struggled as well. Do you remember when Satan tempted Jesus in the wilderness at the very beginning of his ministry? After fasting for forty days and forty nights, Jesus was tempted by Satan to turn stones into bread, throw himself off the temple, and fall down and worship Satan. Jesus refused, but he was sorely tempted. In the garden of Gethsemane, Jesus prayed, "I don't want to do this, God. Let this cup pass from me. Yet not my will but yours be done." Even on the cross, Jesus held out this creative tension. He was crucified between one thief who repented and one who didn't.

When we put righteousness first, which is nothing more than holy living, then everything else in life falls into place. Jesus clearly holds out a vision of discipleship in which we are called to pursue a just, righteous, and holy life. But how do we seek God's kingdom without succumbing to worry about this, that, and the other thing?

The paradox is that there are no easy or simple answers. Every age has to wrestle with what it means to be righteous. Every generation has to agonize about how not to let worry and anxiety so consume us that we are not able to look beyond ourselves to serve others and our world. There is not always one right solution to the question, "How then, shall we live?"

- How can we not worry when we don't have a job?
- How can we not be anxious about tomorrow if our family has no health insurance?
- How can we not look beyond today in order to ensure a future of hope for our children?
- How can we love our enemies when our enemies are not acting justly?
- How can we avoid judging others when they are not living in Christlike ways?

The truth is that, despite what Jesus said, not all birds are adequately fed and not all flowers will bloom. If we live a righteous life, our money problems might not be solved, a job may not magically appear on our front porch, and we may not have the things that we consider necessary for a comfortable life.

Jesus' admonition not to worry is no excuse to be careless, lazy, have a devil-may-care attitude, or rely on blind faith. Nor is Jesus saying we shouldn't be prudent, cautious, or act with forethought. Sometimes it is appropriate to be very concerned about people or issues. Rather, the Greek word used here for "worry" is *merimna*, meaning to worry anxiously.[24] It implies a lack of serenity and an agitated heart. It means that we are so preoccupied with our problems that we cannot even see the birds or smell the flowers. Did you notice? "Worry" is repeated six times in these verses.

Jesus challenges us to look into our hearts and examine our motives and desires. Can we live in day-tight compartments, balancing appropriate concern for the future with living each day fully and with joy? Do we need all that we want? Can we live with enough? Is it possible to make decisions that the world would see as crazy or foolish, believing that God knows what we need? Dare we allow the Holy Spirit to guide us in holy living? Can we embrace the paradox that we are totally dependent on God's grace yet at the same time empowered by the Holy Spirit to strive for righteousness?

In Nepal, I sensed a different ethos, no doubt influenced by Hinduism and Buddhism. There is a calmness among the Nepalese that we frenetic Americans cannot seem to grasp, a sense of peace and equanimity that is undisturbed by stress, hardships, and even danger.

The essential vocational question, then, may not be, "What kind of job do I need to prepare for?" but rather "Who am I? What gifts have I been given? Who has God created me to become?" When we are able to discern our true calling, then we are equipped to make this world a more just and compassionate habitation for all of God's creatures.[25] True vocation joins self and service, as author Frederick Buechner asserts when he defines vocation as "the place where your deep gladness meets the world's deep need."[26]

There's a story about an old, wise spiritual man of India who found a great, precious stone. He carried it in his knapsack. One day he was walking around when a young man rushed up to the old man and said, "Father, last night I had a dream. In this dream, the Almighty One told me that you have in your possession a very beautiful stone: precious, priceless!" The old man wasn't sure what to make of this, whether the young man might just try to steal it from him or even kill him. But he continued the conversation by saying, "Yes, that's true."

The young man ventured a little further. "In the dream, the Almighty One said you might be willing to let me see that precious stone." The old man said, "Of course I will." He reached down into his knapsack, pulled it out, and held it in his hand. The young man took it. You could see in his eyes how he loved it, how impressed by it he was. You could see lights go on in his head as to what having that stone could mean to him. The old religious leader said, "Why don't you take it? I give it to you!"

The young man thought he was kidding. "But, sir, I have no money."

"No, please, take it!" The young man stuck it in his pocket and ran away!

Late that same afternoon, the old man was sitting outside his house saying his prayers when he saw the young man coming toward him. When the fellow got right up to the old man, he said, "Sir, you gave me a very precious gift today."

"That I did," he said.

"Now, sir, I want you to give me an even bigger, more precious gift."

The old man said, "I'm afraid that's the biggest, most precious one I had."

The young man said, "No. You have another one, sir. That's the one I want from you."

"What is it?"

"Sir, I've been thinking about this all day. I want you to give me the gift of giving the most precious thing I have to somebody else."

Every person has at least one area of life that he or she is reluctant to give to God and others. I've counted at least fifteen areas of my life than I won't give up to God, and God and I are in negotiation about five other areas. What is your precious stone? What is it that you have difficulty surrendering to God?

Sometimes the most precious thing we have is our time. We'll give God just about anything but our time. We have other things to do on Sundays. We don't serve on any committees because we're busy on weeknights. And we don't help at the local thrift shop or emergency shelter or food pantry because we'll miss our exercise class. How hard it is for those who have no time for God to enter the kingdom of heaven!

For some, the most precious thing we have is our talents. We may have a variety of skills but prefer to hide our light under a bushel. We may have a lovely singing voice, the gift of relating well to people, or a deep spiritual relationship with Christ but don't use those gifts to reach out to our brothers and sisters with the good news. How hard it is for those who will not offer their talents to enter the kingdom of heaven.

For some, the most precious thing we have is our family. Part of being a parent is helping our children and grandchildren to see beyond their own biological family to God's worldwide family. It's modeling for our children and grandchildren a broader view of the human needs of our world.

In the end, life is not in the taking. Life is not in the scratching, clutching, clawing, cussing, ranting, raving, or getting. No, we are blessed to be a blessing to others. Life is in the surrendering of the most precious thing we have, ourselves, into the hands of God. We give ourselves wholly to God and to others. But how do we live in day-tight compartments and desire first God's kingdom and righteousness in the midst of the problems, challenges, and distractions of everyday life?

What is it that we are keeping for ourselves instead of sharing it with the body of Christ? We build a wall around it, lock it up, and say, "Everything, God, but this! You can have all but this! And I dare you to get it!"

Then, so often, a miracle happens. Jesus, looking at you, loves you. The Holy Spirit starts to work in our lives, and we begin to understand the kind of complete response Jesus asks of us. We are uniquely blessed to be a blessing. Freedom comes by letting go of that which binds us. When our hearts open to the life-changing power of God's love, the fruits of the Spirit pour out into our lives, and we begin to act in new and different ways.

The near loss of my backpack was a sobering example of how much I am attached to and love my things. I was stunned. What would I do without my passport, cell phone, rain jacket, snacks, water, iPad, and journal? I was so impressed by how Rajiv and Bishal handled the situation. They did not panic, they led calmly, and they used collective wisdom to solve the problem. It was a reminder of how important it is for leaders to be able to regulate their emotions in the midst of stress. Our guide showed incredible grace to me despite my huge mistake. Do other people see the grace of Jesus in you during the course of your everyday life as you deal with a myriad of issues?

I also learned a lesson about always being prepared to give up the things I cherish the most. If my backpack had crashed through the branches, we would likely never have been able to recover it, and the trek would have been over. How can I learn to let go of my possessions so that if I would lose everything important to me, I would still be able to rejoice?

> O God, help us to live in day-tight compart-
> ments, offering to you each day all that we
> have and all that we are. And give us the gift
> of giving the most precious thing we have to
> you, to others, and to our world, for with God
> all things are possible.
>
> "The quiet life in day-tight compartments
> will help you to bear your own and others'
> burdens with a light heart."
>
> *(Sir William Osler[27])*

Chapter

5

Many of us are so concerned with our own driven goals and our own survival that we fail to see the "image of God" within our fellow human beings. Like Jesus' teaching of the good Samaritan, . . . only the unexpected one sees a child of God, drops everything, responds compassionately, and gives generously. . . . Namaste. *I began to suspect that Jesus would respond positively to this word.*

Chapter 5
Namaste

Namaste. It's the standard greeting in Nepal, and the word has Hindu origins. It is also a sign of great respect when spoken with hands pressed together in front of the heart and a bowed head. Everywhere I trekked in Nepal, I was greeted with the word *Namaste* without fail. Along with the greeting came a smile.

Namaste literally means "I bow to the divine in you" or "The God in me bows to the God in you." It was an amazing experience of hospitality because I am most accustomed to the rushed way in which Americans pass by many people every day without a word, a smile, or even a glance. I loved greeting and bowing to children, who always yelled out, "Namaste," especially to a person who has a different color skin and a different language.

Now, this required a bit of mental adjustment on my part. As Christians, we don't believe that we are gods. However, we do believe that something of God lives in each one of us because, according to the Book of Genesis, every human being is made in the image of God. The *imago dei* is within us.

My mental framework also shifted from seeing the beauty of Nepal to the tragic destruction of the Gorkha earthquake that devastated central Nepal on April 25, 2015. Our trek took us right through the epicenter of the earthquake, which killed nearly 9,000 people and injured 22,000. The earthquake and its aftershocks also destroyed or damaged 888,000 homes and caused massive destruction of health facilities and schools. The 7.8-magnitude earthquake was the most powerful earthquake in eighty-one years to hit the region.[28]

Landslides destroyed entire villages, and nineteen climbers were killed at Everest Base Camp. In addition, many farms, tourist sites, and guest houses were destroyed, and hundreds of trails were obliterated. Four years later, in the midst of continued rebuilding, an estimated one hundred thousand people are still living in emergency makeshift shelters in Nepal. The economic losses from the earthquake have been estimated to be 10 billion dollars, and reconstruction has been slow.

Within hours of the earthquake, the United States Agency for International Development (USAID) sent a disaster response team to the affected areas to conduct search and rescue and damage assessment, and provide emergency shelter, drinking water, and food. USAID is still highly invested in Nepal, especially in housing reconstruction, and provided over $23.3 million in support for the housing sector as of summer 2017.[29] We frequently saw evidence of USAID's presence during our trek.

The United Methodist Church has also been involved in Nepal for many years as a partner in an ecumenical ministry called United Mission to Nepal. United Methodists around the world have given generously to earthquake relief, knowing that this will be a long-term ministry.

Every day, as we observed evidence of the 2015 earthquake, we also rejoiced in the ongoing rebuilding, and we were humbly grateful for the opportunity to trek in this remote part of Nepal. One night, we actually had the privilege of an indoor private toilet for the first time. The owner of the teahouse said that since so many people were staying at the inn that night, she was opening up the private bathroom adjoining our bedroom. Heaven! Unfortunately, the shower was not connected. Since we had no opportunity to shower yesterday, either, we decided to steer clear of one another during the day.

This was our next to last day before the long and arduous climb to the Larkya Pass, so we did not want to wear ourselves out. Most of the hike was through a beautiful valley. As we were walking and talking among ourselves about the big day tomorrow, Rajiv reminded us that we were combining two days into one in order to complete the entire trek. Then he asked, "Laurie, would you like to ride a horse tomorrow?"

"What? A horse?"

"Yes. I thought maybe you would not want to trek for ten hours. I can arrange that for you."

"Do you think I need a horse?"

"It's just a long day."

We let the issue drop for a while. I consulted Talitha, and she said, "Of course, you can do this. You don't need a horse."

Throughout the entire trek, Rajiv had been reminding us to go slow and steady because it's not a race. So, I said to him, "You've been telling us every day to just go slow and steady, which is what I will be doing tomorrow." Rajiv did not mention riding a horse again.

Even so, I could tell that the air was thinner, and the night before I experienced some sleep disturbance because my breathing was more labored than usual. I lay awake, very aware of the lack of oxygen at this altitude, for the first time wondering whether I could make it through the long day on Friday.

My imagination and anxiety began to run away from me, and I tossed and turned all night. Three more days of hiking total, and today was another short day with a steep 2,000-meter elevation climb. "Lord, have mercy. I am humbled. I am empty. I need you,

God. Give me the strength and energy I need to make it to the pass." I resolved to take it slow and steady and enjoy every moment.

Because of the altitude, we all trekked slowly and stopped frequently for me, the slowest person, to catch my breath. I gained more confidence as we went on, especially after Rajiv said that the ascent tomorrow, while longer, was not as difficult. It is the long downhill after the pass that will be hard on the quadriceps.

We arrived in Dharamsala around 11:30 a.m., which gave us the rest of the day to rest and prepare for the ascent to Larkya Pass the next day. Interestingly, we were put in a room instead of a tent, which we had originally expected. However, the "room" was actually a "cave" since the floor, walls, and roof were all rough-hewn stone. It meant the room was quite cold, so I bundled up in my sleeping bag wearing all my clothes, outer wear, and thermal underwear. Lunch was macaroni and cheese and tomato sauce and a few veggies. Thank you, Jesus, for a little variety of food—truly a taste of heaven!

The afternoon in Dharamsala was miserable. It was drizzly and damp in our cave hotel room, but rest was most important in preparation for the next day. I took a nap and also used the time to read on my iPad. By coincidence, I was in the middle of Scott Parazynski's book, *The Sky Below: A True Story of Summits, Space, and Speed*. Dr. Parazynski is a physician and former astronaut who is a veteran of five Space Shuttle flights and seven spacewalks. He's also a mountaineer who summited 29,029-foot Mount Everest in 2009.

How fascinating that as I lay in my sleeping bag, anticipating crossing the Larkya Pass the next day at 17,060 feet, I was reading about a man who spent several months acclimating himself to the altitude and weather before going for the summit. In 2008 Parazynski made his first attempt but instead ruptured a disc in his lower back and had to abort the summit. Quoting Winston Churchill,

"Success consists of going from failure to failure without loss of enthusiasm," Parazynski tried again the next year and succeeded. Just as people the world over place Tibetan prayer flags at the summits of major peaks in Nepal, so Parazynski brought to the summit multicolored prayer flags to honor astronauts and cosmonauts who had fallen in the line of duty.

Describing how hard it was to keep breathing when every breath was a struggle, Parazynski wrote, "The things in life that come to us the hardest mean the most. Everest has challenged me to the core and nearly broke my back the year before, but I returned, persevered, and made a round-trip to the top. Whenever I find myself down or struggling to solve a problem, my mind goes back to the triumphant moment, and I pick up the pace again."[30]

Navigating in the mountains of Nepal is always an intimidating and dangerous experience and is not for the faint of heart. Of course, the risks are far greater the higher the altitude. More than two hundred mountaineers have died on Mount Everest since 1922, when the first climbers' deaths on Everest were recorded. It is believed that most of the bodies have remained buried under glaciers or snow.[31] In many ways, 2019 was a record-breaking year, with more than 825 climbers and Sherpas reaching the top of Everest. Unfortunately, there were also eleven fatalities in twelve days, including two Americans, with massive overcrowding near the summit as climbers waited hours to get their turn.

The climbing season at Mount Everest is in April and May, and on the few good weather days, there is often a traffic jam since there is only one way up and down. The cost for a permit to summit Everest is $11,000, the total average cost for all expenses related to climbing Everest is around $45,000, and the total time needed is two months. A record 381 climbing permits were issued in 2019.

The reason for the unusual number of deaths in 2019 included a combination of factors. Because of weather, there was a limited number of days when climbers could summit. With the large number of climbers, many remained stuck on a cliff, roped together, and either moving slowly to the top or simply standing still. Because 26,000 feet is in the death zone, the climbers were using up their supplemental oxygen and were slowly and literally "waiting in line to die."

The extreme danger of the situation was described by Jim Davidson, a veteran high-altitude mountain climber who has summited Everest: "When we pass each other, one of us has to unclip from the line in order to get by each other. Trying to cooperate, but you don't speak the same language, you're wearing a mask, it's difficult to talk, so there's constant exposure to danger."[32] Most Everest fatalities occur on the way down from the summit rather than on the way up,[33] likely because of the physical and mental toll of the climb.

Other factors include inexperienced or out-of-shape climbers and unqualified Sherpas who have not been vetted, bad weather, too many permits issued, uneven screening, and corruption. But there is one more variable. Some climbers simply get summit fever. They are so intent on making it to the top that either they disregard basic safety precautions or altitude sickness affects their ability to make good decisions. And, unfortunately, some climbers jockey for position and are not always willing to help fellow climbers who are struggling if it means their own chance to get to the summit is jeopardized.

As I continued to climb the Larkya Pass myself and reflect upon all this, I wondered if it would be possible for the backlog of the climbers near the summit of Mount Everest to take the meaning of Namaste to heart. Many of us are so concerned with our own driven goals and our own survival that we fail to see the "image of God" within our fellow human beings. Like Jesus' teaching of the good Samaritan, the righteous ones pass by a dying human, and only the unexpected one sees a child of God, drops everything, responds compassionately, and gives generously so that the dying man can return to health. *Namaste.* I began to suspect that Jesus would respond positively to this word.

Learning How to Be a Good Neighbor

A legal expert stood up to test Jesus. "Teacher," he said, "what must I do to gain eternal life?"

Jesus replied, "What is written in the Law? How do you interpret it?"

He responded, "You must love the Lord your God with all your heart, with all your being, with all your strength, and with all your mind, and love your neighbor as yourself."

Jesus said to him, "You have answered correctly. Do this and you will live."

But the legal expert wanted to prove that he was right, so he said to Jesus, "And who is my neighbor?"

Jesus replied, "A man went down from Jerusalem to Jericho. He encountered thieves, who stripped him naked, beat him up, and left him near death. Now it just so happened that a priest was also going down the same road. When he saw the injured man, he crossed over to the other side of the road and went on his way. Likewise, a Levite came by that spot, saw the injured man, and crossed over to the other side of the road and went on his way. A Samaritan, who was on a journey, came to where the man was. But when he saw him, he was moved with compassion. The Samaritan went to him and bandaged his wounds, tending them with oil and wine. Then he placed the wounded man on his own donkey, took him to an inn, and took care of him. The next day, he took two full days' worth of wages and gave them to the innkeeper. He said, 'Take care of him, and when I return, I will pay you back for any additional costs.' What do you think? Which one of these three was a neighbor to the man who encountered thieves?"

Then the legal expert said, "The one who demonstrated mercy toward him."

Jesus told him, "Go and do likewise."

(Luke 10:25-37)

The term "good Samaritan" has become part of the vocabulary of millions of people around the world, many of whom have no clue where the phrase originated. It has come to symbolize any person who comes to the rescue of someone who needs help.

We can all look back and identify the good Samaritans in our lives. I remember the frantic days of packing just before my husband, Gary, and I moved from Pentwater to Grand Rapids, Michigan, thirty years ago, when our three children were young. In those days, pastors didn't get any time off between appointments. Gary and I were both full-time pastors, serving separate churches. We were supposed to conclude our ministries on one day in a certain location, start a different ministry in a new location the next day, and somehow get everything packed and moved and not forget the kids and the cats.

On the day the moving van arrived, we were in a panic. All of our stuff was about to be taken out of the house, but some of it wasn't even packed yet. Gary and I thank God for a couple from the church who just showed up on our doorstep that morning, offering to help. These good Samaritans and difference makers completely boxed everything in our garage and packed up much of the basement.

I think of the young man who, other than me, was the only passenger on a commuter plane from Muskegon, Michigan, to Chicago one time. Just two of us. Have you ever been on a plane with just two people? I am not particularly fond of airplanes, especially small ones, and on this day, we were in the middle of a blizzard. This young man sensed that I was near panic, so for the entire one-hour trip across Lake Michigan on that tiny plane in the middle of a blizzard, he talked to me, asked questions, and shared about his life. He never let the conversation lag until we arrived safely in Chicago. I'll never forget the kindness of this good Samaritan and difference maker.

I also remember one time when the West Michigan Annual Conference was at our United Methodist–related Albion College and I took an hour off to go for a run during a lunch break. As I was running along, minding my own business, all of a sudden, I was attacked by a pit bull, who rushed out to the road in search of lunch. I had never seen a pit bull before, but it was around the time when pit bulls were in the news a lot. So I knew I was in deep trouble.

I couldn't outrun him, and I didn't have anything with which to hit him, so I prayed, "Help me, Jesus!" and expected the worst. Then, out of the blue, a teenage boy came running out of the next house with a baseball bat and beat the dog away from me before I was dead meat.

All four of these people were good Samaritans and difference makers. Two of them I didn't know at all, and I have no idea whether they were Christians, but each one was willing to give of themselves to help someone in need.

Of course, the catch is that today we associate Samaritans with "good" people. But in the time of Jesus, Samaritans were a Jew's worst nightmare. The Jews regarded the Samaritans as heretics because they were left behind during the Babylonian exile and intermarried with non-Jews, so they were racially and theologically impure. Samaritans were anything but good. They were the ultimate losers.

This story was prompted by a question from a lawyer, who asked Jesus, "Teacher, what must I do to gain eternal life?" (Luke 10:25). It's important to know that this lawyer was also a theologian, for the only law in which the Jews were interested was the law of Moses. Jesus answered the lawyer's question with another question, "What is written in the Law? How do you interpret it?" (verse 26).

And the lawyer answered, *Love the Lord your God with all your heart, with all your being, with all your strength, and with all your mind, and love your neighbor as yourself* (verse 27). What the lawyer did was combine two key passages from the Jewish law, Leviticus 19:18 and Deuteronomy 6:5. It was an excellent answer, and Jesus told him so, "You have answered correctly. Do this and you will live" (Luke 10:28). But the lawyer wasn't satisfied. He wanted to press the issue further, so he asked another question, "And who is my neighbor?" (verse 29).

The question was not totally unexpected, for it was normal to test the ability of a teacher like this. Furthermore, the problem of who our neighbor is was a very real one for the Jews. For by the time of Jesus, many Gentiles, or non-Jews, had come into Palestine. The question every Jew asked was, "Am I obligated to be a neighbor to the Romans and the Syrians and the Greeks and the Ethiopians or only to other Jews? What are the limits to my circle of love?"

As he often did, Jesus answered with a story. He said, "A man went down from Jerusalem to Jericho. He encountered thieves, who stripped him naked, beat him up, and left him near death" (verse 30).

The seventeen-mile-long road from Jerusalem to Jericho was so dangerous that it was called the "path of blood." For one thing, the road descended from 2,300 feet above sea level in Jerusalem to 1,300 feet below sea level at Jericho, which is right near the Dead Sea, the lowest place on earth. In addition, there were lots of deep ravines, sharp turns, caves, and many places in which to hide.

The first person who passed by this man was a priest. When Jesus mentioned the priest, I'm sure his listeners would have been expecting Jesus to tell how this great man was an example of how to love other people. But, surprise! The priest saw the man and passed by on the other side without stopping. The second person who came upon the beaten man was a Levite. He was similar to a lay pastor or a lay leader in the synagogue. I'll bet Jesus' listeners thought this guy, too, would stop to take care of the man. But he took one glance and moved over to the other side as well.

Why didn't these "good people" stop? Some suggest they were concerned with ritual impurity, but that is unlikely. There was probably more to it. Perhaps they were in a hurry. Maybe the priest had a funeral to conduct, or a wedding to perform, or a service at which to preach. You just can't stop and help someone if that means you will be late, can you? I mean, really. Would you? Or maybe they were unwilling to see this wounded man as worthy of having any claim on their attention. Unfortunately, religious leaders are not always consistent in applying our theology to everyday life.

I'm sure Jesus' listeners were distressed by now. Here were their religious heroes ignoring this man who needed help. Finally, Jesus said, a Samaritan passed by, had pity on the man, and chose to go off the map of culture, expectations, and the law. The good Samaritan chose an alternative, bandaging his wounds, pouring on oil and wine. Then he put the man on his own donkey, took him to an inn, and cared for him. The next day he gave the innkeeper two silver coins, saying, "Take care of him, and when I return, I will pay you back for any additional costs" (verse 35).

This final twist to the story was almost too much for the lawyer and his friends. For here Jesus says that the difference maker, the one who had compassion on the man who was beaten, was none other than a member of a race that the Jews hated bitterly. A person whom the Jews would have unconditionally rejected proved to be a model for the reign of God. I'll bet they thought Jesus was going to say that the Samaritan worked this poor guy over further, that he probably killed him. But no, Jesus forces them to think the unthinkable, that their enemy was the one who did the right thing.

It's easy to see, then, why the lawyer was so taken aback when Jesus asked, "Which one of these three was a neighbor to the man who encountered thieves?" (verse 36). The lawyer couldn't even bring himself to say the word *Samaritan*, so he said instead, "The one who demonstrated mercy toward him." And Jesus said, "Go and do likewise" (verse 37).

Who *is* my neighbor? "Anyone who is in need," Jesus essentially says. *Anyone* who is in need. Have you noticed that the one man we know nothing about in this parable is the one who was beaten? We don't know if he was a Jew or a Samaritan; a Roman or a Greek; a wealthy or a poor man; a good or a bad man; a white, black, Asian, Hispanic, or Native American man; an immigrant; or a transgender person. He was simply a person. He was someone in need, and that was all that mattered.

The second question Jesus addresses in this parable is this: "How can I be a neighbor to others?" What can you do to be a good Samaritan? We become neighbors by looking for God in everyone we meet. We become neighbors by believing that love is more important than fear. If we want to find God, we need look no further than our neighbor.

As you know, we're in a precarious state right now in our country and in The United Methodist Church. At a time when there seems to be so much polarization, people of faith like you and me have to wrestle with the truths that Jesus spoke over and over. If we want to save our lives, we must give them away. If we want to be great, Jesus says, go to the end of the line, sit in the back row, be the last to eat, give away everything that you have, and take care of your enemy. For the last will be first, and the poor will enter the kingdom before the rich.

That's what has been so inspiring as we receive nonstop news in our global world about one disaster or catastrophe after another. Have you noticed? No one asks the person standing on the roof of a flooded house, or trying to escape a wildfire, or fleeing a tornado, all desperate for help, "What's your political party? What's your religion? What's your ethnic identity? Are you an illegal immigrant?" None of that matters. Good Samaritans help people. We are one human family. Our neighbor is anyone in need.

The way you and I make a difference as disciples of Jesus Christ is not only to share the love of Jesus but also to recognize that this good news is countercultural to what our society calls success and getting to the top. For Christ followers, it's about respecting the rights of all, speaking out on behalf of the poor and the oppressed, and shaping a world where every person can live a full and meaningful life.

In The United Methodist Church, we're also in the midst of an uncertain future because of our differences around human sexuality. As we approach the General Conference in 2020, no matter how everything shakes out, I wonder if we dare model a different way of doing and being where we live side by side in the midst of our differences. Dare we vow to see all people as our neighbor, no matter where they live around the world, what language they speak, how they dress, what their gender identity is, or the color of their skin?

My friends, our world desperately needs difference makers for Jesus. Our world desperately needs people who love unreservedly, are continually seeking to become more Christlike, and are committed to unity rather than division. Can we as United Methodists lead the way? Dare we United Methodists take up the mantle of love? Dare we United Methodists be out in front in showing mercy? Dare we United Methodists take delight in finding common ground with those who are not like us? Dare we United Methodists embrace the role of difference makers?

Difference makers are good Samaritans who, out of gratitude, give themselves away in thanksgiving and thanks-living. Each one of you is a shining example of Christ's love and a beacon of hope!

So, Jesus asked the lawyer, which of these three do you think was a difference maker to the man who fell into the hands of the robbers? The lawyer responded, "The one who demonstrated mercy toward him." Jesus said to him, "Go and do likewise."

I can't tell you exactly who your neighbor is. I can't predict to whom you will have an opportunity to be a brother or sister today. And no one can force you to be a good Samaritan. But I do know this: if you walk with the love of God in your heart, eyes open to human need, and ears attuned to the cries of the needy, you will discover your neighbor. And when you minister with faithful love, quiet mercies, and unknown kindness, you will see Jesus in one another. Will you dare to be a good Samaritan?

Chapter
6

Wandering through the mud for hours,
I was reminded that all of us are
peregrini—wanderers through life.
We enter this life bringing nothing, and
we leave this life taking nothing with us.
Essentially, we spend our days on this earth
wandering into grace: grace experienced,
grace embodied, and grace extended
to others.

Chapter 6
The Rest We Have to Take

The alarm went off at 3 a.m. Today is the day! Because of the intense cold of staying in a cave-like room made of stone, the owners were kind enough to give me three extra blankets so that I would not freeze to death. As we continued to climb higher with each passing day, we were also preparing our bodies and minds to crest the Larkya Pass.

I now was experiencing most of the symptoms of altitude sickness, including shortness of breath, headaches, sleep disturbance, nausea, and dizziness. So, while the trek today was a slow, oxygen-depriving, uphill walk to the Larkya Pass, it was doable for me, one step at a time, with the help of the prescription medication Diamox and lots of pauses for rest.

Chicken broth at 4 a.m. did not fill me up, but I was packed and ready with my headlamp to leave in the dark before 4:30 a.m. I kept protein bars accessible in my backpack, knowing that broth alone would not give me the energy I needed. The first hour was unnerving, as we were immediately moving upward. The trail was nothing but stones of every size and shape. Still, one of the most beautiful moments of the trek unfolded along this tortuous path, as, right before sunrise, the clouds parted and we saw Mount Manaslu in all its towering glory. I couldn't help reciting my daily morning prayer again and again.

I rise from my bed of sleep to adore your holy name, to live for you this day, to work with you in the building of your kingdom, and to find in you eternal life. I consciously renew my call as this day begins, thanking you for the privilege of living my life in this way. I know that I need to take care of myself if I am to be of any use to those I am called to serve. Grant me grace to walk in health and wholeness, and, most of all, thank you that I can live today, knowing that I am your beloved. Amen.

I was continually reminded of the privilege I had to walk on top of the world.

As I walked, I remembered that the word *Manaslu* is derived from the Sanskrit word *Manasa*, which means "intellectual" or "soul."[34] The Manaslu Circuit is part of the Nepalese Himalayan region in west-central Nepal and follows an ancient salt-trading route along the Budhi Gandaki River. The first people to summit Mount Manaslu were Japanese climbers Toshio Imanishi and Gyalzen Norbu, who succeeded on May 9, 1956. Many Japanese climbers, in particular, have attempted to summit Mount Manaslu over the years but have failed. Manaslu has been nicknamed "Killer Mountain" because of frequent icefalls and avalanches and its high altitude.

An unspoiled, rarely taken path, the Manaslu Circuit did not open for trekking until 1992. Considered a newcomer to the trekking circuit, Manaslu is known for small teahouses where trekkers can stay overnight as well as purchase an evening meal and breakfast. These teahouses also provide a way to learn more about the region, interact with villagers, and support local economies.

The primary occupation of people in the Manaslu region is

animal husbandry and agriculture, especially barley, corn, oats, and nuts. Most of the local people in the villages we passed through are of Tibetan origin, speak various dialects, and are either Hindu or Buddhist. The houses in this particular region are unique in that the walls are built with stones and the roofs with stone slabs.

During our trek, we did not see many animals. We shared our trails most frequently with groups of donkeys carrying supplies from one high mountain village to another. They were mostly herded by young men, all of whom had cell phones! Our modern world leaves no region untouched. In one village where we stayed, we also saw a huge herd of yak. The domesticated yak is indigenous to the Himalayan region, and their dried droppings are an important source of fuel in the higher elevations of Nepal and Tibet. In addition, yak meat, butter, milk, and cheese are all eaten in Nepal.

Other wild animals found in this region include the grey wolf, Himalayan musk deer, blue sheep, Asian black bear, langur monkey, and over 110 species of birds. Thirty-three species of mammals and some reptiles are also found. Hunting is banned in the area where we were trekking.

Rajiv, Bishal, Talitha, and I made a few strategic decisions as we headed out for the Larkya Pass. Halfway through the trek, I had started carrying Talitha's tripod in my backpack so that we could all have the best weight distribution. An outstanding amateur photographer, she wanted to take advantage of this unique opportunity to use the tripod and telephoto lens for night shots and sunsets.

Since I was the slowest trekker, on this day we decided to let Rajiv carry the tripod in order to lessen the weight I carried. It was a good decision because the higher we trekked, the more difficult it was to catch my breath. Of course, the magnificence of watching the sun rise over Manaslu and seeing the soaring panorama of the Himalayan range was enough to take even more of my breath away!

The hike was not as vertical as yesterday. Even so, I discovered that it helped to stop every several hundred steps or so to calm my breathing before taking the next several hundred steps. Eventually, Rajiv asked if he could carry my backpack for a little while so that it would be even easier for me. Since his own pack was on his back, Rajiv put my now infamous red backpack across his chest. What a gift Rajiv gave to our team because I was now walking faster.

Every time I looked around, I saw new vistas that threatened to further take my breath away. A glacial lake, pure blue, with the sun reflecting off the water, and a string of mountains in every direction. How, I wondered, was I so privileged to take in such beauty that few other people will ever be able to experience because there are no roads?

Rajiv had suggested a few days before that I might not be able to make it to the Larkya Pass, at an altitude of 17,060 feet, but, to his surprise, I did it! One step after another, huffing and puffing, gulping in air, slowly ascending to the pass on a glorious morning—but I made it. It took four hours, and we arrived at the top around 8:30 a.m.

I am nearly incapable of describing the feeling of standing at the Larkya Pass, surrounded by the vast array of Himalayan peaks while Nepalese prayer flags waved in the wind. Every flag told a story of courage, every flag a testimony to the determination, commitment, and toughness of each person who stretched beyond his or her own capacity to make it to the pass.

A prayer flag is a colored cloth left by trekkers on mountain peaks. Trekkers in Nepal, Tibet, and other countries put them on high mountain peaks in order to bless the surroundings. The flags often include holy mantras (sayings), and the tradition is that whenever the wind blows, these mantras travel through air.

My eyes filled with tears as I realized how few people have the training or experience to make it all the way. Talitha and I both left our personal prayer flags at the pass. We also noticed that dozens of cairns had been fashioned out of the billions of rocks just lying around, waiting to be used. I also made a cairn, which is a human-made pile of stones, intended to be a sign of the presence of the divine.

Since ancient times, cairns have traditionally been used as memorials, landmarks, or direction markers. If you make a habit of paying attention to your surroundings, you will see cairns all over the world. I build cairns in most places that I travel because, for me, they are a sign of God's presence, grace, and hope in our world. They are also a symbol of the spiritual journey to which God invites all of us, regardless of the faith that we profess.

The four of us took a selfie at the pass and congratulated one another with Snickers bars, a rare treat that we saved just for this occasion. The scriptures I carried with me today were, "Carry each other's burdens and so you will fulfill the law of Christ" (Galatians 6:2) and "Come to me, all you who are struggling hard and carrying heavy loads, and I will give you rest" (Matthew 11:28). How do you and I help each other share our burdens?

As I gave thanks for the deep privilege of making it to the Larkya Pass and for Rajiv, who graciously carried my pack for part of that time, I also remembered the heavy burdens I had carried over the past two years as a rookie bishop. Because the responsibilities of a bishop are so weighty, it is critical to also carve out opportunities to let go of everything.

In Nepal, where I was completely off the grid, I was free to focus solely on the next step and the thirteenth commandment not to fall. It also gave me the freedom to be my true self. I had so much fun with Talitha, and it was an incredible gift to share two and a half weeks together. Plus, for lunch today we had cheese for the very first time in Nepal. I wondered if it was yak cheese.

However . . . we were not yet done. The weather was perfect all the way up, but we had six more hours of downhill trekking before reaching our overnight stop. When we finally arrived at the teahouse, Talitha and I ordered a bucket of hot water so we could wash off after three days of no showers. How grateful we were for this simple blessing. Again, I didn't sleep well and struggled with my breathing. Even though we were not at 17,000 feet anymore, we were still at a high elevation, and my body was still stressed by the intensity of the trek.

Rajiv told us that the last day of our trek would be a piece of cake after yesterday. Unfortunately, he was wrong. Completely wrong. I don't fault Rajiv because I suspect he may have never before led groups on the Manaslu Circuit in July because the trail was officially closed. It rained hard during the night, and when we left at 7:00 a.m., the first half hour of the trek was gorgeous. We walked along a river with a full view of the majestic Mount Manaslu in front of us.

Then we hit the mud and rocks. Oh my! I flashed back to the first two days of the trek when I wasn't even sure I would be able to continue.

I said, "Rajiv, what's going on here? I'm wandering in a wilderness of mud."

"Well, it looks a little messy."

"Did you know this trail would be muddy? I thought we were done with these treacherous conditions."

"I guess we're not done. Just be careful and go slow," he said. "It's going to take us longer to get to the teahouse than I thought."

Actually, it would take us hours longer. We were going to finish up with a marathon of mud!

We slogged hard for three solid hours in conditions that were even worse than the first two days. I usually prefer to know ahead of time what to anticipate so that I can adjust my expectations and be prepared. To be honest, I was ready to be done and did not want to have to focus this hard simply to stay upright. One time in the morning, I slid down a large rock but otherwise was okay. I didn't dare ask Rajiv how long the mud would entrap us because if I knew, it might push me over the edge.

My key words for the morning were *Balance*, *Concentrate*, and *Smile*. Thank God for trekking poles to keep me upright. This is clearly not what I had hoped for on the last day when we were so near the end. Of course, Rajiv had no idea what the conditions would be, so he and Bishal went ahead at their own paces. Meanwhile, Talitha and I wandered our way through the mud in a thick forest, not even sure where the trail was at times. It reminded me of how The United Methodist Church is moving into an unknown future where everything seems to be messy and off-kilter.

I admit that it was appealing to just lie down in the mud and have a tantrum. I mean, we made it to the pass. We thought the last day would be a piece of cake, but it turned out to be the most challenging and difficult of all. Am I going to make it to the end? It was time for my mantras to kick in. When participating in long-distance runs or triathlons, I use mantras to motivate myself when I am tempted to just lie down in the road or along the trail and give up. Over and over, I say to myself, "I am a lean, mean running machine. I am a strong, confident cyclist. I can glide through the water like a fish."

We trekked for five hours and twenty minutes before stopping for lunch. Resting in a beautiful, isolated mountain village, I knew that I could not endure another six-plus hours if mud and slippery rocks were involved. At the same time, I refused to give in to the fear that I wouldn't be able to make it to the end of the trek. Pastor/writer/storyteller Michael E. Williams wrote in *The Upper Room Disciplines: A Book of Daily Devotions 2019*, "God does not want us to be enslaved to a spirit of fear, a spirit that keeps us from doing what we are asked to do by God. Like my mother, God is watching over us to comfort us and give us courage as we make the journey through the darkness, through our fear, to what God asks us to do."[35]

To bolster my confidence and pass the time, I added up in my head all the steps that we took in the past twelve days. With a conservative estimate of 25,000 steps a day, I suspect we will have taken 300,000 steps, which is more than a quarter of a million steps.

Here I was, trekking in the most difficult of conditions, and I took 300,000 steps with only two slips and no major falls (unless I count my backpack fiasco). Yet, just a week before leaving for Nepal, I took a three-mile run out on the Missouri prairie and fell and broke my wrist. The learning for me is to always be mentally, emotionally, and physically prepared for whatever comes my way each day. I was bound and determined that the awful conditions of the last day would not destroy my spirit.

Wandering through the mud for hours, I was reminded that all of us are *peregrini*—wanderers through life. We enter this life bringing nothing, and we leave this life taking nothing with us. Essentially, we spend our days on this earth wandering into grace: grace experienced, grace embodied, and grace extended to others.

It is God's grace that goes before us, however. It is a grace that prepares the way for us to respond to God's call, even in the midst of the instability of many of our lives. God's love is always out in front, calling us to claim ourselves and others as beloved children of God and empowering us to make a difference in a world that is not always kind or fair.

In the end, it's the journey itself that matters. I wonder: Is it possible to be called to a wanderer's life of discovery and hope? Are we willing to ramble out of our comfort zone into the mud and muck of life, where so many in our world struggle simply to survive? Can we let go of the many things that distract us daily from our call to be bearers of grace, mercy, and hope in our world? And how does God meet us along the path, where the destination does not matter as much as the journey itself?

This ended up being the longest trekking day of all, a total surprise, demanding all of our concentration, energy, and determination not to give up. "Ever-present God, help me to know that you are watching over me so that I will not be enslaved by my fear."[36]

Mercifully, later in the morning, the terrain became a little more forgiving, we made better time, and I was more optimistic that we could finish strong and in a good frame of mind. After ten hours, we proudly trekked into Dharapan Heaven's guest house and restaurant. It was a long, dirty, muddy, steep grind. Even as we passed through gorgeous scenery and a few lovely villages, it was tough, but there was also a feeling of accomplishment, having reached the goal without giving up. And best of all? We were able to take hot showers.

We spent the entire next day making our way back to Kathmandu, which was one last adventure. Hiring a jeep to take us halfway to Kathmandu, Talitha and I squeezed into the left front seat (in Nepal driving is on the left side of the road), which was a bit bone crushing and nerve-wracking, but it also gave us a chance to see the landscape. We were stopped for a while by a landslide cleanup and drove right through a pretty good-sized river.

Transferring to another car, we became stuck in a massive two-hour traffic jam on the outskirts of Kathmandu, where both the traffic and the pollution are mind-boggling. It was a stark reminder of the beauty of the trail we had traversed and our responsibility as followers of Jesus to take our faith and hope back into a world where joy is often in short supply.

Our minds contained sweet memories of the trail, and our hearts were full. Rajiv and Bishal, one a Hindu and the other a Buddhist, were wonderful guides and traveling companions. Our spirits are at rest, and our minds and bodies are at peace. God is good, and all is well. Namaste.

Learning How to Take the Rest We Need

"Come to me, all you who are struggling hard and carrying heavy loads, and I will give you rest. Put on my yoke, and learn from me. I'm gentle and humble. And you will find rest for yourselves. My yoke is easy to bear, and my burden is light."
(Matthew 11:28-30)

Do you know how to take the rest that you need to rejuvenate yourself? Do you know when to stop? Do you know how to say no? I confess that I work way too hard. I admit that I often put my job above family and self. I acknowledge that, more often than not, I am out of balance and am not leading a whole and healthy life. One of the reasons I decided to travel to Nepal was to be completely away from work and the sources of work stress, including that from my computer and cell phone.

Mark Twain (1835–1910), pen name for Samuel Langhorne Clemens, was a writer, humorist, entrepreneur, lecturer, and publisher. In 1869, Twain wrote and published a travel book called *The Innocents Abroad, or The New Pilgrims' Progress*. The book chronicles what Twain called his "Great Pleasure Excursion" with a group of Americans on a chartered boat through Europe and the Holy Land in 1867. Twain writes,

> Afterward we walked up and down one of the most popular streets for some time, enjoying other people's comfort and wishing we could export some of it to our restless, driving, vitality-consuming marts at home. Just in this one matter lies the main charm of life in Europe—comfort. In America, we hurry—which is well; but when the day's work is done, we go on thinking of losses and gains, we plan for the morrow, we even carry our business cares to bed with us, and toss and worry over them when we ought to be restoring our racked bodies and brains with sleep. We burn up our energies with these excitements, and either die early or drop into a lean and mean old age at a time of life which they call a man's prime in Europe. When an acre of ground has produced long and well, we let it lie fallow and rest for a season; we take no man clear across the continent in the same coach he started in—the coach is stabled somewhere on the plains and its heated machinery allowed to cool for a few days; when a razor has seen long service and refuses to hold an edge, the barber lays it away for a few weeks, and the edge comes back of its own accord. We bestow thoughtful care upon inanimate objects, but none upon ourselves. What a robust people, what a nation of thinkers we might be, if we would only lay ourselves on the shelf occasionally and renew our edges![37]

Already, 150 years ago, Mark Twain was noticing what may be one of the greatest threats to health and happiness in our country: overwork. Overwork leads to all kinds of physical, emotional, relational, and psychological problems. Twain laments that Americans cannot give it a rest! We are continually worrying about tomorrow, fussing about money, obsessed with status, and oblivious to the truths that we learn from the earth: "When an acre of ground has produced long and well, we let it lie fallow and rest for a season." When was the last time that you rested for a season?

The fourth of the Ten Commandments (Exodus 20:8-11) says,

Remember the Sabbath day and treat it as holy. Six days
you may work and do all your tasks, but the seventh day is a
Sabbath to the LORD your God. Do not do any work on it—
not you, your sons or daughters, your male or female servants,
your animals, or the immigrant who is living with you.
Because the LORD made the heavens and the earth, the sea,
and everything that is in them in six days, but rested on the
seventh day. That is why the LORD blessed the Sabbath day
and made it holy.

If God took a break and rested on the sabbath, don't you think we should, too? The kind of rest that I am talking about is holy rest. It is rest that rejuvenates our spirits, renews our minds, strengthens our bodies, and gladdens our hearts. I used to think rest was a waste of time. I'd say to myself, "If I rest, I'm not doing anything. And if I'm not doing anything, I'm disappointing God because there are so many needs in this world. So many people are carrying heavy burdens. So many people need a listening ear, a gentle touch, or an encouraging word. I can't afford to rest."

If God didn't make it clear enough in the Ten Commandments that we need to rest, Jesus made sure we knew. From the very beginning of his ministry, Jesus intentionally took time to go away and be by himself to rest and pray. Already in chapter 1 of Mark, we read, "Early in the morning, well before sunrise, Jesus rose and went to a deserted place where he could be alone in prayer" (verse 35). In chapter 3, "Jesus left with his disciples and went to the lake. A large crowd followed him because they had heard what he was doing" (verse 7). In chapter 6, Jesus said to his disciples, "Come by yourselves to a secluded place and rest for a while" (verse 31). Later in that chapter, Jesus sent the people away and climbed a mountain to pray (verses 45-46). And in chapter 7, Jesus entered a house in Tyre where he didn't think he would be found, but later he discovered he couldn't hide (verse 24).

As it was with Jesus, so it's difficult for you and me to stop. It's not easy to say no. It's tempting to work at a pace that seems to get faster with each passing year. Unfortunately, it's also a pace that will eventually make us sick, give us compassion fatigue, or burn us out if we do not follow Jesus' example and rest. After taking time away for renewal in 2001, 2011, and 2018, I now know that rest is not a waste of time. It's holy time. It's a life-giving opportunity for growth and maturity.

Unfortunately, there have been a number of times over the thirty-eight years of my ministry when my compulsion to keep working and the inability to stop and rest have caused me to become sick. Several times I have developed pneumonia or other infections that have literally put me into bed, despite my insistence that I had to keep going.

Our episcopal residence in the Des Moines metropolitan area is on top of a hill in a subdivision, and I am able to be outside on the balcony when the weather is nice. In winter, I can sit at the kitchen table and look outside as I work. A few months ago, when there was still snow on the ground, it suddenly occurred to me.

There are no leaves on the trees right now. It's winter. Everything outside is dead—or is it?

We know that what we see of a tree is only half of that tree. There is as much of the tree below the ground as there is above the ground. That's amazing when you think of it, isn't it? In the winter, the tree looks dormant. Nothing's happening. But, in fact, it's in winter that the tree grows its roots and finds new sources of water and nourishment. More than that, how much the roots of a tree grow in the dormancy of winter determines how much the branches of that tree will grow, blossom, and flower in the summer.

It's that way for us as well, isn't it? Just like a tree, there is as much inside our spirits as there is on the outside. There is as much in our root system as there is on the exterior. Just as a tree needs a time of dormancy in order to grow its roots, so we need rest in order to grow our spirits. We need rest so that when summer comes, we, too, can bloom and flourish. We need rest so that the depth of our roots can provide the stability we need in order to cope when burdens arrive at our doorstep. It is when we intentionally pause that we grow in invisible ways and receive the nourishment that we need in order to live healthy, fulfilled lives. Jesus offers us holy rest. Jesus wants us to come to him and learn from him.

But there is a second part to this scripture. "Take my yoke upon you, and learn from me; for I am gentle and humble in heart, and you will find rest for your souls. For my yoke is easy, and my burden is light" (Matthew 11:29-30 NRSV). Why can we come to Jesus? Because Jesus is gentle and humble in heart. We don't have to be afraid. We don't have to hesitate, and we don't have to feel guilty. Jesus is waiting with open arms to receive us and our burdens.

Some of us, however, don't come to God because we don't feel worthy. We think God disapproves of us or is disappointed by our supposed lack of faith. I suspect that says more about us than it says about God. The good news is that we can know who God is through Jesus Christ. Jesus came to this earth to show us that God is pure love. God always wants the best for us. God is always gentle and humble.

The word *humble* derives from the root word *humus*, which means "ground."[38] Jesus was one of us. Jesus was the Son of God, yet he was also human, made out of the clay of the earth. In the words of spiritual writer Wendy Wright,

> To be humble is to balance midway on the spiritual tightrope between the knowledge of our extraordinary blessedness and our very real brokenness. Psalm 8 says we are created a little less than God. Yet we are also humus, clay. We are wounded, marred, frail. To be humble means that we understand our real humanness, our earthiness into which divine life is poured. At the meeting between human and divine is where we find the spiritual life.[39]

And it is where we find holy rest.

Jesus also says that he is gentle. *Gentle* can be defined as gracious, kind, and free from harshness or sternness. We humans are led to the love of God, not by force, argument, or debate but by gentle persuasion. Rather, we love people to Christ. Anything that is not gentle, such as pressure, impatience, judgment, severity, and shouting—I don't think it works. I think Jesus is saying here that when we learn from him to be gentle and humble, not only do we find the secret of holy rest but also we become examples to others who are desperately looking for a way to carry their heavy burdens.

There's one more thing. Jesus talks about a yoke. He says, "Take my yoke upon you. . . . For my yoke is easy, and my burden is light" (Matthew 11:29-30 NRSV). A yoke is a wooden bar that connects two animals around their necks so that they can work together as a team. The best yokes are custom-made to fit a particular animal. As a trained musician, I have often sung the oratorio *Messiah* by George Frideric Handel, and I remember vividly the chorus, "His Yoke is Easy." The lightness of the soaring lines of the soprano part always reminds me of how, when we are yoked with Christ, we are able to make a positive difference in our world in ways we had never thought possible.

There is a legend saying that Jesus, in the carpenter shop of Nazareth, made the finest yokes in all of Galilee. People from all over the country came to Jesus to buy the best yokes skill could make. In those days, as now, shops had their signs over the door. It has been suggested that the sign above the carpenter's door in Nazareth could have read, "My yoke fits well."[40]

So, Jesus says to each one of us today, "My yoke fits you very well. The life I give you is not a burden that will paralyze you. It's not a task that is utterly overwhelming. You don't have to carry the weight of your worries by yourself. Rather, the intentions I have for your life fit your needs and abilities exactly. When you learn from me and are gentle and humble, the yoke fits well. And when that burden becomes heavy, come to me, lay yourself on the shelf, and I will renew your edges."

Trekking in Nepal provided the mental rest that I desperately needed. For my entire life, I have put my whole self into ministry, regardless of where I was appointed. And in the last few years, the demands of being an episcopal leader have become almost impossible to fulfill. In The United Methodist Church across our worldwide connection, we have been facing declining churches, financial viability, the challenge of being a global church, racism and sexism, and the necessity of changing the way we do ministry in today's world. In addition, we seem to be impossibly divided over human sexuality, with little hope that we can choose to honor our differences in the big tent that could be United Methodism.

Perhaps the greatest challenge is not to try to bear the burden of our denomination, thus becoming a "quivering mass of availability," which is a term Richard Lischer coined in his memoir about serving as a young pastor of a country church, *Open Secrets: A Memoir of Faith and Discovery*.[41] To over-function and try to satisfy everyone's wants and needs in lieu of strategic decision-making about what is most important for creating healthy, outwardly directed organizations is a recipe for failure.

At the same time, as Christ followers we are yoked together for mission and ministry around the world in the Wesleyan tradition. Jesus even claims that this yoke is easy to bear and that the burden is a sheer joy! Dare we make a commitment to continue a yoking of some sort in order to most effectively share the good news of Jesus Christ with a world that desperately needs to know of Christ's love? Could it be that the rest we have to take is a rest from anything that gets in the way of God's light shining through us? Even though the future is uncertain, I am convinced that leading with grace and kindness as well as clarity and accountability in such a time as this demands emotional intelligence, humility, and a deep sense of discovery as well as hope, knowing that God always goes before us.

By choosing to be a *peregrina* and engaging in a trek that demanded considerable physical and mental energy, I wasn't just exchanging one task for another. Rather, by laying myself on the shelf and claiming the rest I had to take, I was able to let go of everything else and simply hang out with God on top of the world for a brief moment and be renewed.

Postscript

Knowing how critical it is to receive the spiritual food that God offers; making a commitment to travel lightly; and letting go of physical, mental, and emotional baggage beckon me to turn outward in service to our communities and the world.

Postscript

Wandering into Grace

Our God is a wandering God. God wanders the world as a *peregrino*, seeking, beckoning, and wooing us into a life of faith and servanthood. Our place of grounding is not a physical location. Rather, we are grounded in relationship with Jesus and other people. We are grounded in love, grace, and hope. And we are grounded in the conviction that wherever God leads, we are called to follow with anticipation, faith, and joy.

Because we are all on a journey of grace, the church, then, becomes our community of faith where we journey together. By no means do we all think the same. However, we are united by our common witness to God's love, justice, and mercy. Grace always leads the way, accompanies us on the journey, and follows behind to catch us when we fall.

The months after returning from Nepal have been the most challenging that I have experienced in thirty-eight years of ministry. Our denominational struggles around human sexuality have exacted a toll on clergy and laity alike and have compromised our single-minded commitment to mission, witness, and ministry to our world.

After the special called General Conference in 2019 in St. Louis, some have wondered if there is a future for them in The United Methodist Church. Others have feared that The United

Methodist Church has lost its way because we are obsessed with one issue and are ignoring the weightier matters of justice and mercy. In many ways, The United Methodist Church reflects the extreme polarities of our political system in the United States.

My broken wrist and the splint that I wore for the entire trek in Nepal continue to remind me of my own brokenness as a disciple of Jesus Christ who is called to be an episcopal leader for such a time as this. As a *peregrina* on a pilgrim journey, I am convinced that wandering into and embodying grace in a fractured world is the best witness that we can offer to our faith. In the end, our true home is in God.

I learned many things from the kindness of my friends in Nepal and the sheer beauty and majesty of the land itself. Foremost was patience. Embracing active waiting and rest as spiritual disciplines will continue to teach me into the future. Immersing myself in Nepalese culture has enabled me to see more clearly how our American culture of intensity and drive is not healthy for many (or any!) of us.

Even so, using the simple RAD process (Reflect, Adjust, Do) prompted my daughter and me to make wise decisions that affected every aspect of our trek and offered a blueprint for continual improvement. By having to face my fears and stretch beyond my limits, I gained more confidence in myself and tapped into the potential that lies within each one of us to change the world.

I continue to facilitate Come to Jesus meetings and value the importance of sitting at table together to reflect on difficult challenges. Knowing how critical it is to receive the spiritual food that God offers; making a commitment to travel lightly; and letting go of physical, mental, and emotional baggage beckon me to turn outward in service to our communities and the world.

Learning about Buddhism and Hinduism is a reminder that Christ also calls me to empty myself in order for God to use me as a difference maker in the world. I am still learning the value of Namaste, the spiritual gift of seeing the goodness of God in all people and treating one another with dignity and respect.

Most of all, I have learned that wandering into grace may be somewhat haphazard and unplannable, but it is also our calling. It is a life we choose. When we stretch ourselves beyond our limits and have the courage to move out of our comfort zone, it is always grace that leads us home. Namaste.

Questions for
Reflection

Questions for Reflection

Questions for Chapter 1:
Reflect, Adjust, Do

1. The ability to adapt to a rapidly changing world and church is a critical skill. We are called to continually RAD (reflect, adjust, do) all of our plans and actions without accusation or blame. How is critical reflection, collaboration, and the courage and flexibility to switch directions essential to wise decision-making in your life?

2. How does your church do transformative ministry by discovering both its strengths and limitations and being willing to adapt creatively?

3. David was an unlikely vessel of God's grace who defeated Goliath by strategically compensating for his weaknesses. What do you think about Malcolm Gladwell's counterintuitive statement that "we learn more from compensating for our weaknesses than capitalizing on our strengths"?

4. How does the spiritual discipline of waiting call us to be attentive and sharpen our focus?

5. Has there ever been a time when you have "fallen upward"?

Questions for Chapter 2:
The Come to Jesus Meeting

1. Have you ever had the experience of someone else second-guessing and making assumptions about your abilities, experiences, or knowledge?

2. Has there ever been a time when you knew that you needed to have a Come to Jesus meeting with another person but were reluctant to be honest about your concerns?

3. Are there times when we are too "nice" in the church, thereby allowing bad behavior to continue?

4. How does taking the initiative to build authentic and transparent relationships break down barriers?

5. In what ways can the church model for the world how to negotiate in good faith in order to move forward?

Questions for Chapter 3:
You Must Eat More!

1. How do we teach and preach that the bread of life that sustains all of us is free, no strings attached?

2. If the bread of life is for all, what does that mean for The United Methodist Church in our struggle to determine who is truly welcome in the church?

3. How can the church offer physical as well as spiritual bread to a hurting world, which includes both the very rich and the very poor?

4. On the Manaslu Circuit, we could not effectively complete our daily treks without food because we expended an enormous amount of energy every day. In the same way, effective clergy and lay leaders in our churches must offer spiritual food to our congregations that will sustain their spirits and empower them to reach out to our world in witness, grace, and love. How will you fortify yourself for the journey, and how will you model Christ's love to those who hunger and thirst for meaning and hope?

5. If the World Cup can bring people together from across the globe, how is God calling us as people of faith to be catalysts for unity and creating a world where all people have a roof over their heads and food on the table?

Questions for Chapter 4:
It's Just a Backpack

1. I wandered myself into grace on the day my backpack tumbled over the edge of the trail. Our guide and porter had every right to be furious with me. I was irresponsible, and they were responsible for our welfare; yet they demonstrated grace. Can you think of a time when you received grace upon grace?

2. What does it mean for you to live in day-tight compartments?

3. How does this quotation speak to you? "Change being inherent in life, disappointments and disasters are likely to happen, and when they do come, we should meet them with equanimity and a balanced response."[42]

4. What is your precious stone? What is the one thing that is almost impossible for you to surrender or let go of and prevents you from living a full life?

5. How have the losses in your own life strengthened your faith and anchored your hope?

Questions for Chapter 5:
Namaste

1. How might The United Methodist Church and our world be transformed if we looked for God in every person we meet? What might happen if we greeted every person we met by bowing our heads, pressing our hands in front of our hearts, and saying the words, "God's peace be with you"?

2. Mission is at the heart of The United Methodist Church. It is imperative for church leaders to connect congregations to God's work around the world by sharing stories of lives being changed through mission and outreach and also providing opportunities for Christ followers to let their lives speak by committing their time, energy, financial resources, and prayers to hands-on mission. How can we as individuals and as congregations embody grace as we live out our mission to make disciples of Jesus Christ for the transformation of the world?

3. Knowing that we are all bound together by our common humanity, how does grace empower us to rebuild hope and trust in The United Methodist Church, our country, and our world in the midst of partisan politics at home and among nations?

4. Who is your neighbor?

Questions for Chapter 6:
The Rest We Have to Take

1. What is the rest that we have to take as leaders and people of faith in order to be effective and fruitful over the long haul?

2. How can leaders allow others the grace to catch their breath before the next task?

3. Are we as Christ followers willing to share and carry the burdens of others?

4. How can we avoid over-functioning and being a quivering mass of availability?

5. How can the church be a place of discovery and hope?

Acknowledgments

Acknowledgments

The opportunity to travel and to write is a precious gift. I would not have been able to trek in Nepal had it not been for the commitment of The United Methodist Church to health and wholeness for its leaders. I am grateful for a denomination that provides opportunities for clergy and bishops to take renewal leaves away from their church responsibilities. Having the time to wander, discover, wonder, rest, and restore mind, body, and spirit enables clergy to return to their ministry settings with vision, hope, and a renewed sense of call.

Wandering into Grace is the result of the support and encouragement of many people. I am grateful to my husband, Gary, for his insights, edits, and partnership. My daughter Talitha was a constant companion whose patience, good humor, and hiking experience kept me going (and laughing) when the going was tough.

Without the expertise and guidance of our guide, Rajiv, and porter, Bishal, Talitha and I would have never found the trail, let alone completed the trek. And my editor, Maria Mayo, was both diligent and gracious in keeping me on track and offering ways to enhance the narrative.

If not for the love and prayers of friends, colleagues, and family, we might still be wandering in the Himalayas. Even as I return home to active ministry, I remain a *peregrina*, with no destination other than to model the suffering love of Jesus, seek justice and reconciliation, and offer hope to all. I continue to be grateful for the tender mercy of God's love, the unfailing grace of Jesus Christ, and the fierce sweetness of the Holy Spirit, which sustains me along the Way.

Notes

Notes

Introduction

1. Rueben P. Job, *A Guide to Retreat for All God's Shepherds* (Nashville: Abingdon Press, 1994), 14.
2. Kathleen Norris, *Dakota: A Spiritual Geography* (Boston: Houghton Mifflin, 1993), 16.

Chapter 1: Reflect, Adjust, Do

3. "Veriditas Pilgrimage at Ghost Ranch, NM," Veriditas, https://www.veriditas.org/ghostranch.
4. See Richard Rohr, *Falling Upward: A Spirituality for the Two Halves of Life* (San Francisco: Jossey-Bass, 2011).
5. Paul Brunton, "Chapter 5: Grace," no. 262, in *The Notebooks of Paul Brunton: The Reverential Life* (Category 18), Paul Brunton Philosophic Foundation, https://paulbrunton.org/notebooks/18/5.
6. Dan Schawbel, "Malcolm Gladwell: The Truth About How David Beat Goliath and How You Can Too," *Forbes*, October 1, 2013, https://www.forbes.com/sites/danschawbel/2013/10/01/malcolm-gladwell-the-truth-about-how-david-beat-goliath-and-how-you-can-too/#2015679157c3.
7. Schawbel, "Malcolm Gladwell."
8. Schawbel, "Malcolm Gladwell."
9. A teahouse is a basic and rustic form of accommodation for trekkers in Nepal and often includes a bed, dinner, and breakfast.

Chapter 2: The Come to Jesus Meeting

10. Carl Dudley, Theresa Zingery, and David Breeden, "Insights Into Congregational Conflict," ed. David Roozen, Faith Communities Today, https://faithcommunitiestoday.org/wp-content/uploads/2019/01/Insights-Into-Congregational-Conflict.pdf.
11. "The Metaphor of the Well," JustPeace, https://justpeaceumc.org/the-metaphor-of-the-well/.

Chapter 3: You Must Eat More!

12. Amelia Merchant, "10 Facts About Poverty in Nepal," The Borgen Project, September 11, 2018, https://borgenproject.org/ten-facts -about-poverty-in-nepal/.

13. "Roti, the Nepali Flat Bread," Boss Nepal, http://bossnepal.com /roti-the-nepali-flat-bread/.

14. Lauren Winner, *Wearing God: Clothing, Laughter, Fire, and Other Overlooked Ways of Meeting God* (New York: HarperOne, 2015), 113.

15. Paul R. La Monica, "The Buzz: Nobody Puts Barbie in a Corner. Mattel Soars," CNN Business, February 2, 2016, https://money .cnn.com/2016/02/02/investing/mattel-earnings-barbie/index .html.

16. Robert Farrar Capon, *Between Noon and Three: Romance, Law, and the Outrage of Grace* (Grand Rapids, MI: Wm. B. Eerdmans, 1997), 7.

17. *The Merriam-Webster.com Dictionary*, s.v. "companion (*n.*)," https:// www.merriam-webster.com/dictionary/companion.

18. "Gallup 2019 Global Emotions Report," Gallup, https://www .gallup.com/analytics/248906/gallup-global-emotions-report -2019.aspx.

19. Niraj Chokshi, "Americans Are Among the Most Stressed People in the World, Poll Finds," *The New York Times*, April 25, 2019, https://www.nytimes.com/2019/04/25/us/americans-stressful .html.

20. Chokshi, "Americans Are Among the Most Stressed People."

Chapter 4: It's Just a Backpack

21. *The World Factbook*, s.v. "Nepal," https://www.cia.gov/library /publications/the-world-factbook/geos/print_np.html.

22. William Montgomery McGovern, *An Introduction to Mahāyāna Buddhism* (New York: E. P. Dutton & Co., 1922), 8, HolyBooks .com, https://www.holybooks.com/an-introduction-to-mahayana -buddhism/.

23. *Langholm Old Church Parish Magazine*, No. 59, January 1966, Langholm Archive Group, http://www.langholmarchive.com /parishmags/jan66.php.

24. "Bible Commentaries: William Barclay's Daily Study Bible; Matthew 6" StudyLight.org, https://www.studylight.org/ commentaries/dsb/matthew-6.html.

25. Parker J. Palmer, *Let Your Life Speak: Listening for the Voice of Vocation* (San Francisco: Jossey-Bass, 2000), 16.

26. Frederick Buechner, *Wishful Thinking: A Seeker's ABC* (San Francisco: HarperSanFrancisco, 1973), 119.

27. William Osler, *A Way of Life: An Address to Yale Students Sunday Evening, Sunday Evening, April 20, 1913* (London: Constable & Company, 1913), 60.

Chapter 5: Namaste

28. Kathryn Reid, "2015 Nepal Earthquake: Facts, FAQs, and How to Help," updated April 3, 2018, World Vision, https://www.world vision.org/disaster-relief-news-stories/2015-nepal-earthquake -facts.

29. "Nepal: Post-Earthquake Housing Reconstruction Support," updated August 9, 2017, United States Agency for International Development (USAID), https://www.usaid.gov/nepal/fact-sheets /post-earthquake-housing-reconstruction-support.

30. Scott Parazynski and Susy Flory, *The Sky Below: A True Story of Summits, Space, and Speed* (New York: Little A, 2017), 225.

31. Bard Wilkinson, "Glacier Melt on Everest Exposes the Bodies of Dead Climbers," CNN, updated March 21, 2019, https://www .cnn.com/2019/03/21/asia/everest-glacier-dead-bodies-scli-intl /index.html.

32. "Veteran Mountain Climber Details Crowded Conditions, 'Constant Exposure to Danger' on Mount Everest," CBS News, May 29, 2019, https://www.cbsnews.com/news/mount-everest -summit-traffic-congestion-climbers-deaths-nepal-mountain/.

33. Massachusetts General Hospital, "Why Climbers Die on Mount Everest," ScienceDaily, December 15, 2008, https://www.sciencedaily.com/releases/2008/12/081209221709.htm.

Chapter 6: The Rest We Have to Take

34. "Manaslu, a Wonderland: 10 Facts That Will Amaze You," Nepal Sanctuary Treks, https://www.nepalsanctuarytreks.com/manaslu-amazing-facts/.
35. Michael E. Williams, "Awaiting the Spirit," in *The Upper Room Disciplines: A Book of Daily Devotions 2019* (Nashville: Upper Room Books, 2018), 191.
36. Williams, "Awaiting the Spirit," 191.
37. Mark Twain (Samuel L. Clemens), from Chapter XIX in *The Innocents Abroad, or The New Pilgrims' Progress*, Project Gutenberg's *The Innocents Abroad*, last updated May 25, 2018, http://www.gutenberg.org/files/3176/3176-h/3176-h.htm.
38. *The American Heritage Dictionary of the English Language*, s.v. "humble (*adj.*)," https://ahdictionary.com/word/search.html?q=humble.
39. Wendy Wright, "Little Things: a Meditation in Three Parts," *Weavings* XVIII: 1 (Jan–Feb 2003): 12–21.
40. "Bible Commentaries: William Barclay's Daily Study Bible; Matthew 11" StudyLight.org, https://www.studylight.org/commentaries/dsb/matthew-11.html.
41. Richard Lischer, *Open Secrets: A Memoir of Faith and Discovery* (New York: Doubleday, 2001), 67.

Questions for Reflection

42. Robert Bogoda, "Buddhist Culture, The Cultured Buddhist," in *Collected Bodhi Leaves, Volume 5*, no. 139 (Kandy, Sri Lanka: Buddhist Publication Society, 2013), 242, https://books.google.com/books?id=mAVCDwAAQBAJ&pg=PA242&lpg=PA242&dq#v=onepage&q&f=false.